MLPAO MLA/T Certification Exam:
Practice Test 2

’;

First published in 2020

This edition was published on November 5, 2024

This work is not created or endorsed by the Medical Laboratory Professionals' Association of Ontario (MLPAO)

Visit Examelot's site at **examelot.com**

ISBN 9798697738979

MLPAO MLA/T Certification Exam: Practice Test 2

Examelot

Contents

Hi! I'm Merlin, the question wizard of Examelot. Welcome to this second book of practice questions for the MLPAO MLA/T exam!

This book contains 500 practice questions for the MLPAO MLA/T exam, divided into the thirteen competencies of the exam. You can find the answers at the end of each section.

If you have any issues or concerns, send the Examelot team an email at **contact@examelot.com**.

Good luck in your MLPAO MLA/T exam!

Merlin

About the MLPAO MLA/T exam

Introduction

The MLPAO MLA/T Certification Exam is a test that students must pass to work as laboratory assistants in Ontario, Canada. The exam is administered by the Medical Laboratory Professionals Association of Ontario (MLPAO).

Eligibility

You can take the MLPAO MLA/T exam if you have graduated from an MLA/T program in Ontario in the last five years.

If you're currently enrolled in an MLA/T program in Ontario, you can still apply for the exam as long as you finish your program before the exam date.

If you don't meet these eligibility criteria, you may still be able to take the exam. You'll need to email documents proving your relevant education or work experience (such as a resume, letter from an employer, diplomas, and degrees) to exam@mlpao.org. The MLPAO will determine if you have enough academic and clinical experience to take the exam.

Exam dates

The MLPAO MLA/T exam is held four times per year: in March, June, September, and November. For the latest exam dates, visit www.mlpao.org/mlat-exam.

Registration closes approximately two months before each exam date.

Registration

To register for the exam:

1. Go to mlpao.org/mlat-exam, scroll down, and click the register button
2. Enter your contact information
3. Choose the applicable exam fee
4. Choose if you want to take the exam at home or a testing center
5. Pay the exam fee by credit or debit card
6. Email your supporting documents to the exam@mlpao.org. In most cases, this is your MLA/T diploma. The MLPAO will also accept a letter from your school confirming your completion date.

TIP

Apply for the exam early (3–4 months before the exam date) for an early registration discount of $100.

Exam fee

The exam fee varies based on whether:

- you're a member of the MLPAO
- you're taking the exam at home or at a testing center
- you're a student or graduate
- you register for the exam early

The lowest exam fee is $210 for student MLPAO members taking the exam at home, while the most expensive exam fee is $615 for special consideration candidates taking the exam at a testing center. For the specific exam fees, see www.mlpao.org/mlat-exam.

TIP

If you're a student in an MLA/T course, join the MLPAO to reduce the exam fee by $165. Student membership to the MLPAO costs just $24. To join the MLPAO, visit mlpao.org/membership. The discount only applies to students.

Taking the exam

There are two ways to take the exam:

- At home
- At a testing center in Ontario

Most people prefer to take the MLPAO exam at a testing center instead of at home. Testing centers have reliable equipment and internet, so there's less chance of technical problems. Plus, you don't have to worry about setting up your room for the exam. You simply show up, sit down at a computer, and get started. Overall, testing centers make the exam experience less stressful.

Taking the exam at home

If you decide to take the exam at home, the MLPAO will email you instructions on how to book your exam around three weeks before the exam date. This email will also contain your exam login information.

Before your exam day, you should make sure your computer to meets the minimum requirements:

- a computer or laptop (not a tablet, smartphone, or Chromebook) with a microphone, speakers, and webcam
- a reliable internet connection
- Windows 8 (or higher) or MacOS 10 (or higher)
- the Guardian Secure Proctoring Browser (which you can download from guardian.meazurelearning.com)

On exam day, you'll need to be in a private, well-lit room with a clear workspace. Make sure to close all programs on your computer except for your web browser. You'll then be assigned an online proctor who will verify your room setup via webcam. Once everything is set, your proctor will unlock the exam, and you'll be ready to begin. The proctor will monitor you throughout the exam.

What you'll need on exam day

On the exam day, ensure you have:

- your government-issued photo ID
- your unique MLPAO Exam ID (if you're taking the exam at home)

What you can't use on exam day

The following items are not allowed during the exam:

- Calculators (you will have access to a virtual calculator during the exam)
- Paper
- Pens or pencils
- Notes
- Phones
- Smart watches

Drinks are allowed but food is generally not permitted.

Passing the exam

The exam has 200 multiple-choice questions. You will need to correctly answer at least 60% of the questions to pass.

What if I fail the exam?

If you fail the MLPAO MLA/T exam on your first attempt, you can retake it within 1 year.

If you fail the exam on your second attempt, the MLPAO will send you instructions on how to become eligible to retake the exam. This will include doing refresher coursework.

The maximum number of times you can attempt the exam is three.

Cancelling the exam

If you need to cancel your exam, email the MLPAO at mlpao@mlpao.org to get a refund of the exam fee, minus the application fee and a $50 administrative fee.

Make sure you cancel at least 30 days before the exam date. Otherwise, you won't get a refund.

Competencies

The questions on the MLPAO MLA/T exam cover thirteen competencies, each testing a different area of knowledge about laboratory work. The thirteen competencies are:

1. Standards of Practice
2. Medical Terminology
3. Basic Biology, Anatomy and Physiology
4. Laboratory Mathematics and Quality Assurance
5. Specimen Procurement, Processing and Data Collection
6. Laboratory Safety
7. Laboratory Equipment
8. Histology and Cytology
9. Clinical Microbiology
10. Clinical Chemistry
11. Clinical Hematology
12. Transfusion Medicine
13. Electrocardiograms

The following table shows the percentage distribution of the competencies assessed in the MLPAO exam.

Table 1: Percentage distribution of the competencies in the MLPAO exam.

Competency	Percentage of exam
Standards of Practice	8–10%
Medical Terminology	5–7%
Basic Biology, Anatomy and Physiology	4–6%
Laboratory Mathematics and Quality Management	8–10%
Specimen Procurement, Processing and Data Collection	12–16%
Laboratory Safety	12–16%
Laboratory Equipment	5–7%
Histology and Cytology	4–6%
Clinical Microbiology	7–9%
Clinical Chemistry	8–10%
Clinical Hematology	8–10%
Transfusion Medicine	3–5%
Electrocardiograms	5–7%

The next few pages will describe each of the thirteen competencies in detail.

1. Standards of Practice

The first competency, Standards Of Practice, is worth 8–10% of the MLPAO exam and includes questions about:

- Laws regulating laboratories

- Canada Health Act
- Health Care Consent Act, 1996
- Laboratory and Specimen Collection center Licensing Act, Regulations 682 & 683
- Occupational Health and Safety Act
- Ontario Regulation 107/96 Controlled Act
- Personal Health Information Protection Act (PHIPA)
- Personal Information Protection and Electronic Documents Act (PIPEDA)
- Regulated Health Professions Act (RHPA), 1991 (especially section 11)
- Transportation of Dangerous Goods (TDGS) Act
- Workplace Hazardous Materials Information System (WHMIS)

- Patient confidentiality
- Quality management
- Ethics
- The roles, responsibilities, and behaviour expected of lab assistants and lab technicians

2. Medical Terminology

The second competency, Medical Terminology, is worth 5–7% of the MLPAO exam. It will test your knowledge of medical terms such as:

- Prefixes (e.g. -endo, -epi, -hypo)
- Suffixes (e.g. -cyte, -ectomy, -lysis)
- Root words (e.g. adip/o, carcin/o, lapar/o)
- Directional terms (e.g. anterior, posterior, dorsal)
- Medical terms

3. Basic Biology, Anatomy & Physiology

The third competency is Basic Biology, Anatomy & Physiology. This competency is worth 4–6% of the MLPAO exam and includes questions about:

- Blood
- Body cavities (skull, thorax, abdomen, and pelvis)
- Body systems:
  - Lymphatic
  - Digestive
  - Respiratory
  - Nervous
  - Urinary
  - Reproductive
  - Endocrine
  - Immune
- Bones
- Organs (brain, heart, lungs, liver, stomach, intestines, skin, etc.)
- Muscles
- The human cell
- Tissues

4. Laboratory Mathematics and Quality Assurance

The fourth competency, Laboratory Mathematics and Quality Assurance, is worth 8–10% of the MLPAO exam and includes questions about:

- Laboratory mathematics
  - Conversion from Fahrenheit to Celsius and vice versa
  - Dilution calculations
  - Exponents
  - International System (SI) units

- Ratios, proportions, and dilution
- Significant digits and rounding off
- Statistics (mean, median, and standard deviation)
- The metric system
- Quality control
  - Accuracy and precision
  - Sources of error
  - Standards and controls
- Chemical grades
  - Analytical
  - Technical
  - Commercial
  - C.P.
  - USP
  - B.P.
  - Certified ACS
- Types of water
  - Deionized
  - Distilled
  - Grades of water defined by the CLSI

5. Specimen Procurement, Processing, and Data Collection

The fifth competency is Specimen Procurement, Processing, and Data Collection. The competency is worth 12–16% of the MLPAO exam and includes questions about:

- Vacutainer additives
  - Anticoagulants (EDTA, sodium citrate, heparin, potassium oxalate, sodium polyanethol sulfonate)
  - Clot activators (silica, etc.)
  - Glycolysis inhibitors (sodium fluoride)
  - Plasma separating gel
  - Serum separating gel

- Venipuncture equipment
  - Vacutainers
  - Needles
  - Needle gauges
  - Butterfly needles
  - Lancets
  - Microtubes
- Venipuncture techniques
  - Identifying the patient
  - Identifying the correct site for blood collection
  - Applying the tourniquet
  - Decontaminating the skin
  - Entering the needle into the vein
  - Order of draw
  - Releasing the tourniquet
  - Inverting the tubes
  - Complications (e.g., fainting, bruising, hematoma)
- Collection and storage of feces
  - Culture and sensitivity (C&S)
  - Fecal occult blood (FOB)
  - Fecal fat
  - Ova and parasites (O&P)
  - Viral studies
- Collection and storage of urine
  - Mid-stream urine collection
  - 24-hour urine collection
- Collection and storage of other specimens
  - Semen
  - Skin
  - Sputum
- Transportation of specimens
  - Category A and Category B
  - Chain of custody
  - Specimen preservation
- Serum/plasma separation
- Test priorities (stat, urgent, routine)
- Critical values

6. Laboratory Safety

The sixth competency is Laboratory Safety. This competency is worth 12–16% of the MLPAO exam and will ask you questions about:

- Safety laws
  - Canadian Nuclear Safety and Control Act
  - Hazardous Products Regulations
  - Occupational Health and Safety Act
  - Transportation of Dangerous Goods Regulations
  - WHMIS 2015
- Transporting dangerous goods
  - Risk Groups (1, 2, 3, and 4)
  - Category A and Category B
  - Classes of dangerous goods
  - Packaging requirements
  - Packaging labelling requirements
- Safe laboratory practices
- Control of biological hazards (pathogens, patient fluids, aerosols)
  - Biological safety cabinets
  - Containment levels
  - Decontamination
  - Safety pipette fillers
  - Sharps containers
  - Universal precautions
- Control of chemical hazards
  - Chemical labels
  - Cleaning of chemical spills
  - Emergency shower
  - Eyewash station
  - Fume hoods
  - PPE
  - Safety data sheets
  - Safety symbols
  - Spill kit

- Storage of chemicals
- Control of physical hazards (fire, compressed gas, cryogenic fluids, electricity)
  - Fire extinguishers
  - Flammable storage cabinets
- Control of radiation hazards
  - Protective equipment
  - Cleaning radioactive spills
- Waste disposal (chemical, biological, biomedical, and radioactive)
- First aid procedures for:
  - chemical burns
  - choking
  - CPR
  - electric shock
  - exposure to patient body fluid
  - exposure to radioactivity
  - heart attack
  - heat burns
  - needle stick injuries
  - trauma

7. Laboratory Equipment

The seventh competency is Laboratory Equipment. This competency is worth 5–7% of the MLPAO exam and covers laboratory equipment such as:

- General equipment
  - Autoclaves
  - Balances
  - Centrifuges
  - Freezers
  - Glassware
  - Hot plates
  - Microscopes
  - PH meters
  - Plasticware
  - Refrigerators

- Spectrophotometers
- Thermometers
- Water baths

- Hematological equipment
  - Cell counters
  - Hemocytometers
  - Microhematocrit centrifuge
  - Sedimentation tubes
- Microbiological equipment
  - Automated media processors
  - Biosafety cabinets
  - Culture media (plates and tubes)
  - Hot air ovens
  - Incubators
- Histological equipment
  - Automatic cover slip applicator
  - Coverslippers
  - Cryostats
  - Cytospins
  - H&E stainers
  - Microtomes
  - Tissue processors
- Urinalysis equipment
  - Automated strip readers
  - Reagent strips
- Biochemistry equipment
  - Automated chemistry analyzers
  - Blood gas analyzers
  - Desiccators
  - Ion-exchange resin
  - Water distillers
- Transfusion equipment
  - Cell washers
  - Heating blocks
  - Serofuges
- Phlebotomy supplies
  - Biohazard containers
  - Needles
  - Tubes

8. Histology and Cytology

The eighth competency is Histology and Cytology. This competency is worth 4–6% of the MLPAO exam and will ask you questions about:

- Histology
  - Accessioning
  - Fixation
  - Decalcification
  - Tissue processing
  - Staining
  - Coverslipping
  - Slide filing
  - Tissue block filing
- Cytology
  - Accessioning
  - Fixation/preservation
  - Centrifugation
  - Cell block preparation
  - Cytocentrifuge
  - Direct smear preparation
  - Liquid-based processors (e.g. ThinPrep, SurePath)
  - Staining
  - Coverslipping (manual and automated)
  - Slide filing
- Specimen rejection criteria
- Cross-contamination risks and procedures

9. Clinical Microbiology

The ninth competency is Clinical Microbiology. This competency is worth 7–9% of the MLPAO exam and it will ask you questions about:

- Bacteria, viruses, parasites, protozoa, and fungi
- The terms normal flora, opportunist, commensal, and pathogen
- Organism Risk Groups (1, 2, 3, and 4)
- Collecting specimens (urine, CSF, etc.) for microbiology
    - Tube additives
    - Tube colours
- Transporting specimens for microbiology
    - Transport media
- Handling specimens
- Agar media (preparation and storage)
    - Blood agar
    - McConkey agar
    - Chocolate agar
    - Thayer Martin agar
    - Phenyl ethyl alcohol (PEA) agar
    - Salmonella-shigella (SS) agar
    - Thioglycolate broth
    - CLED
    - Hektoen enteric agar
- Agar slant tubes
- Culture broth tubes
- Automated agar plate streakers
- Incubation of specimens
    - Incubation conditions (temperature, oxygen requirements)
    - The terms aerobic, anaerobic, microaerophilic, etc.
    - Anaerobic jar
    - Anaerobic glove box
    - CO_2 incubator
    - Candle jar
- Staining
    - Gram stain
    - Acid-fast stain
    - Fluorescent stains
    - Fluorescent antibody stains
- Bacteria
    - The difference between gram-positive and gram-negative
    - The difference between cocci and bacilli
- Autoclaving

10. Clinical Chemistry

The tenth competency, Clinical Chemistry, is worth 8–10% of the MLPAO exam and includes topics such as:

- Urinalysis
    - Urine collection (routine and microscopic, 24-hour)
    - Rejecting unacceptable urine specimens
    - Preparing urine for microscopic examination
    - Measuring 24-hour urine volume
    - Preserving urine specimens
- Glucose tolerance testing
    - Administrating glucose solutions
    - Handling adverse reactions
    - Timed blood sample collections
- The purpose and normal ranges for the following tests:
    - Cardiac markers
    - Drug levels
    - Electrolytes
    - Endocrine function
    - Glucose testing

- Hepatitis testing
- Lipid profiles
- Liver function
- Renal function
- Tumor markers
- Automated biochemistry analyzers

11. Clinical Hematology

The eleventh competency is Clinical Hematology. This competency is worth 8–10% of the MLPAO exam and will ask you questions about:

- Hematology terms (e.g. leukocytosis, leukopenia, thrombocytosis, thrombocytopenia)
- Specimen requirements and rejection criteria
- Hematology analyzers
  - Automated cell counters
  - Automated coagulation analyzers
  - Counting chambers
- The meaning and normal ranges for:
  - blood differential test
  - hematocrit
  - hemoglobin
  - MCH
  - MCHC
  - MCV
  - platelet count
  - PT, PTT and INR
  - red blood cell count
  - white blood cell count
- How to recognise and manage blood samples that are:
  - agglutinated
  - clotted
  - hemolyzed

- icteric
- lipemic
- Manual techniques
  - Preparation of blood films
  - Reticulocyte counts
  - Sedimentation rate (how to set up an ESR, the difference between Westergren and Wintrobe methods)
  - Staining
- Other hematology tests
  - Factor assays
  - Platelet function tests
  - Hemoglobin determinations

12. Transfusion Medicine

The twelfth competency is Transfusion Medicine. This competency is worth 3–5% of the MLPAO exam and covers topics such as:

- Blood donations
  - Collecting blood (anticoagulants, additives)
  - Tests performed on blood donations (hepatitis B, hepatitis C, HIV, etc.)
  - Criteria for specimen rejection
- Blood products
  - Cryoprecipitated AHF
  - Granulocytes
  - Plasma
  - Platelets
  - Red cells
- Storage of blood products
- Tests to prevent transfusion reactions
  - ABO grouping
  - Rh typing
  - Antibody screening and testing

13. Electrocardiograms

The final competency is Electrocardiograms.
This competency is worth 5–7% of the MLPAO
exam and will ask you questions about:

- Preparing a patient for an ECG
- Placing the ECG leads on the patient
- Operating the ECG
- Maintaining ECG equipment
- Correcting ECG artifacts
- Holter monitors

Practice questions

Competency 1

Standards of Practice

There are 20 questions in this competency.

1.1 Which principle of the Canada Health Act is not patient-focused but the means of achieving the other four principles?
   a) Accessibility
   b) Comprehensiveness
   c) Portability
   d) Public administration
   e) Universality

1.2 Which of these is the responsibility of a laboratory assistant?
   a) Disciplining workers
   b) Giving results to patients
   c) Performing tests that require judgement
   d) Preparing chemical solutions
   e) Supervising other workers

Answers on page 22

1.3 A lawyer asks a lab technician for copies of his client's test results. What should the lab technician do?

a) Allow the lawyer to see the results on the computer

b) Give the results to the lawyer immediately

c) Have the lawyer sign a Medical Release Form and then release the results

d) Have the lawyer sign a confidentiality form and then release the results

e) Tell the lawyer to contact the physician who ordered the tests

1.4 A phlebotomist draws blood for a pregnancy test. After the woman has left the room, a colleague approaches the phlebotomist and asks what test was ordered. He explains he wants to know because he is the woman's ex-boyfriend. The phlebotomist should:

a) call the police

b) inform his colleague he has no right to know which test was ordered

c) lie and tell his colleague the test was a complete blood count

d) reassure his colleague that he has nothing to worry about

e) tell his colleague the test was a pregnancy test

1.5 Another term for professional negligence is:

a) defamation

b) malfeasance

c) malpractice

d) misfeasance

e) nonfeasance

1.6 What is Canada's federal data privacy law for private-sector organizations?

a) HIPPA

b) PHIPA

c) PIPA

d) PIPEDA

e) WHMIS

Answers on page 22

1.7 Who enforces PIPEDA?

   a) Health Canada

   b) Information and Privacy Commissioner of Ontario

   c) Ministry of Health

   d) Privacy Commissioner of Canada

   e) Public Health Ontario

1.8 The Regulated Health Professions Act, 1991 is legislation that:

   a) establishes the conditions that health insurance plans must meet to receive cash contributions

   b) governs Ontario's regulated health professions' Colleges

   c) governs the personal information handling practices of federal government institutions

   d) outlines the behaviour expected of health professionals

   e) sets the primary objective of Canadian health care policy

1.9 Which Ontario act sets the rights and duties of workers and establishes the procedures for dealing with workplace hazards?

   a) Excellent Care for All Act

   b) Health Care Consent Act

   c) Laboratory and Specimen Collection Centre Licensing Act

   d) Occupational Health and Safety Act

   e) Regulated Health Professions Act

1.10 In Ontario's Occupational Health and Safety Act, a 'competent person' is a person who:

   a) can make informed decisions about his or her health care

   b) follows the current CSMLS Standards of Practice guidelines

   c) has worked in their position for more than 10 years

   d) has worked in their position for more than 5 years

   e) is qualified because of knowledge, training, and experience

Answers on page 23

1.11 Which of these is a 'controlled act' within the Regulated Health Professions Act (RHPA)?
a) Drawing blood from a patient
b) Praying for a patient
c) Shaking a patient's hand
d) Sneezing into your arm
e) Weighing a patient

1.12 The Health Care Consent Act is about patient consent to:
a) confidentiality
b) disclose health information
c) privacy
d) publication of their data in medical journals
e) treatment

1.13 Which government organization legislates the Laboratory and Specimen Collection Centre Licensing Act?
a) Canadian Healthcare Association
b) College of Medical Laboratory Technologists of Ontario
c) Ministry of Health
d) Ontario Health
e) Public Health Agency of Canada

1.14 According to Regulation 682 of the Laboratory and Specimen Collection Centre Licensing Act, a medical lab technician is a person:
a) responsible for administrating technical and scientific lab operations
b) responsible for supervising other workers in the laboratory
c) who may perform specialized scientific tests without supervision
d) who performs tests that require independent judgement
e) who performs tests that require limited skills and responsibility

Answers on page 23

1.15 What does PHIPA do?

    a) Control the use of confidential information at the federal level

    b) Control the use of confidential information at the provincial level

    c) Manage informed consent

    d) Protect employees

    e) Protect minorities

1.16 What is the purpose of the Canada Health Act?

    a) To ensure all Canadian residents have access to necessary health care

    b) To ensure all health workers in Canada work in a safe environment

    c) To eradicate dangerous diseases from Canada

    d) To protect confidential patient information

    e) To provide health care services for people who can pay for the services

1.17 The accessibility principle of the Canada Health Act states:

    a) Canadians must have reasonable access to healthcare facilities

    b) a Canadian who moves to a different province is still entitled to coverage

    c) all printed health materials must be made accessible in Braille

    d) anyone in Canada can register for free healthcare, regardless of immigration status

    e) healthcare facilities must be accessible to people with disabilities

1.18 Which PIPEDA principle allows anyone to ask organizations for a copy of their personal information?

    a) Accountability

    b) Consent

    c) Individual Access

    d) Openness

    e) Safeguards

Answers on page 23

1.19 Which act is Canada's federal legislation for publicly funded health care insurance?

a) Canada Health Act

b) Established Programs Financing Act

c) Hospital Insurance and Diagnostic Services Act

d) Insurance Companies Act

e) Medical Care Act

1.20 Under the Canadian Constitution, which level of government is responsible for the direct health care services of First Nations living on reserves, Inuit and Innu populations, veterans, and inmates of federal prisons?

a) Local

b) District

c) Municipal

d) Provincial and territorial

e) Federal

Answers on page 24

ANSWERS

1.1 d) Public administration

Public administration is a principle of the Canada Health Act that requires provincial and territorial health care insurance plans to be operated on a non-profit basis by a public authority. While this principle is not directly patient-focused, it ensures the other four principles (universality, comprehensiveness, accessibility, and portability) are achieved through a publicly managed system.

1.2 d) Preparing chemical solutions

Preparing chemical solutions is the task of a laboratory assistant. Laboratory assistants perform basic tasks such as preparing solutions, handling specimens, and maintaining equipment.

Supervising workers, giving results to patients, and performing tests requiring judgment are typical responsibilities of more advanced laboratory personnel, such as technicians, technologists, and managers.

1.3 e) Tell the lawyer to contact the physician who ordered the tests

Laboratory technicians can only give results to the physician who ordered the tests. Release of test results to third parties, including lawyers, can only be done by the physician or patient. Even then, the physician would need authorization from the patient before providing the lawyer with a copy of the results.

1.4 b) inform his colleague he has no right to know which test was ordered

You should only share health care information on a need-to-know basis. In this case, the ex-boyfriend does not have the right to know which tests were ordered.

1.5 c) malpractice

In law, malpractice is an instance of negligence or incompetence by a professional. It is also known as professional negligence.

1.6 d) PIPEDA

PIPEDA is the Personal Information Protection and Electronic Documents Act, a Canadian law that sets out the rules for how businesses must handle personal information in the course of their commercial activity.

HIPPA is the Health Insurance Portability and Accountability Act, which is United States privacy law, not Canadian law.

PHIPA is the Personal Health Information Protection Act, which is a privacy law in Ontario.

PIPA is the Personal Information Protection Act, which is a privacy law in British Columbia.

WHMIS is the Workplace Hazardous Materials Information System, Canada's system for dealing with dangerous materials in the workplace.

1.7 d) Privacy Commissioner of Canada

PIPEDA is a federal privacy act. The Privacy Commissioner of Canada is responsible for enforcing PIPEDA.

1.8 b) governs Ontario's regulated health professions' Colleges

In Ontario, many health professions are self-governed by Colleges. The Regulated Health Professions Act governs these Colleges.

1.9 d) Occupational Health and Safety Act

The Occupational Health and Safety Act (OHSA) protects workers from hazards in the workplace. It does this by setting out worker rights, the duties of all workplace parties, and the procedures for dealing with workplace hazards.

1.10 e) is qualified because of knowledge, training, and experience

The Occupational Health and Safety Act defines a competent person as someone who:

1. is qualified because of knowledge, training, and experience to organize the work and its performance,
2. is familiar with the act and the regulations that apply to the work, and
3. has knowledge of any potential or actual danger to health or safety in the workplace.

1.11 a) Drawing blood from a patient

Any procedure performed below the dermis, such as phlebotomy, is a controlled act.

1.12 e) treatment

The Health Care Consent Act (HCCA) is an Ontario law that has to do with the capacity to consent to treatment.

1.13 c) Ministry of Health

The Laboratory and Specimen Collection Centre Licensing Act is legislation specific to Ontario. It is legislated by the Ministry of Health, the ministry responsible for administering Ontario's health care system.

1.14 e) who performs tests that require limited skills and responsibility

Specifically, Section 1 of Regulation 682 says "laboratory technician means a person who under direct supervision performs laboratory tests which require limited technical skill and responsibilities".

1.15 b) Control the use of confidential information at the provincial level

PHIPA (the Personal Health Information Protection Act) is the privacy law in Ontario.

1.16 a) To ensure all Canadian residents have access to necessary health care

The Canada Health Act ensures that all eligible residents of Canada have reasonable access to insured health services without direct charges at the point of care.

1.17 a) Canadians must have reasonable access to healthcare facilities

The accessibility principle of the Canada Health Act ensures that all residents of Canada have reasonable access to medical care without financial or other barriers.

1.18 c) Individual Access

The principle of Individual Access under PIPEDA (Personal Information Protection and Electronic Documents Act) gives everyone the right to access personal information held about them by an organization.

1.19 a) Canada Health Act

The Canada Health Act is the legislation that governs Canada's publicly funded health care system. It sets the standards for universal, accessible, and comprehensive health care across all provinces and territories.

1.20 e) Federal

The federal government is responsible for providing direct health care services to specific groups, including First Nations people living on reserves, Inuit and Innu populations, veterans, and inmates of federal prisons.

Competency 2

Medical Terminology

There are 35 questions in this competency.

2.1 What does hypertrophy mean?
a) Excess energy
b) Increase in cell numbers
c) Increase in size
d) Newborn
e) Underdeveloped

2.2 What is the term for the contraction phase of the heartbeat?
a) Diastole
b) Pacemaker
c) Septum
d) Systole
e) Tachycardia

2.3 What is phagocytosis?
a) An abnormally high number of phagocytes in the blood
b) An abnormally low number of phagocytes in the blood
c) An autoimmune disease where phagocytes attack the body's own cells
d) The process by which phagocytes engulf foreign material
e) The process by which phagocytes move

Answers on page 33

2.4 What is the common abbreviation for the Papanicolaou test?

    a) D-dimer test

    b) P-test

    c) PPN test

    d) Pap test

    e) Polymerase test

2.5 Glycolysis is the breakdown of:

    a) glucose

    b) glycogen

    c) glucagon

    d) glycerol

    e) glycosylate

2.6 What is the term for the production of blood cells and platelets?

    a) Apheresis

    b) Apheresynthesis

    c) Coagulation

    d) Hemopoiesis

    e) Hemosynthesis

2.7 White blood cells are also known as:

    a) erythrocytes

    b) leukocytes

    c) lipocytes

    d) osteocytes

    e) thrombocytes

2.8 A thrombus is a:

    a) instrument for measuring blood pressure

    b) moving foreign body in the bloodstream

    c) type of blood clot

    d) type of blood vessel

    e) type of needle for aspirating pleural fluid

Answers on page 33

2.9 What does the prefix brady- mean?

    a) Different

    b) Hidden

    c) Same

    d) Slow

    e) Together

2.10 Which does the prefix adeno- refer to?

    a) Glands

    b) Joints

    c) Kidney

    d) Liver

    e) Muscle

2.11 What does the suffix -emia refer to?

    a) Blood condition

    b) Eating disorder

    c) Enlargement

    d) Paralysis

    e) Surgical removal

2.12 Which suffix means "tumor" or "mass"?

    a) -algia

    b) -emia

    c) -oma

    d) -osis

    e) -tomy

2.13 In clinical chemistry, what does PSA stand for?

    a) Partly-specific antibody

    b) Patient safety awareness

    c) Plasma-specific antibody

    d) Platelet-specific antigen

    e) Prostate-specific antigen

Answers on page 33

2.14 QNS stands for:

    a) quality not satisfied

    b) quality not sufficient

    c) quantity not satisfied

    d) quantity not sufficient

    e) questionable node suspected

2.15 ETS stands for _____ _____ system.

    a) electrical tube

    b) evacuated tube

    c) extra thrombosin

    d) extravascular testing

    e) extravascular tube

2.16 In the context of healthcare, what does CBC stand for?

    a) Center for blood care

    b) Center for blood control

    c) Complete blood count

    d) Complete blood culture

    e) Controlled blood count

2.17 Small red or purple spots caused by a minor hemorrhage are called:

    a) palachiae

    b) parachiae

    c) parasites

    d) pasachiae

    e) petechiae

2.18 What is edema?

    a) A bruise on the head

    b) A build-up of wax in the ear

    c) A collection of blood outside blood vessels

    d) Swelling caused by fluid retention

    e) The final product of the blood coagulation step in hemostasis

Answers on page 34

2.19 What is a fistula?
  a) A build-up of pus in body tissue
  b) A knot of old scar tissue
  c) A vein that has become distended and engorged
  d) An abnormal connection between two parts of the body
  e) An infection of the large intestine

2.20 What is a hematoma?
  a) A cancer of the blood that originates in red blood cells
  b) A cut in the skin
  c) A localized collection of blood outside the blood vessels
  d) A part of a blood clot that breaks off and travels to a new part of the body
  e) A severed artery

2.21 What is hematuria?
  a) A clotting disorder
  b) A skin rash
  c) Bacteria in the bloodstream
  d) Blood in the urine
  e) Kidney stones

2.22 What is the medical term for a low level of glucose in the blood?
  a) Hyperglycemia
  b) Hyperinsulinemia
  c) Hyperlipidemia
  d) Hypodermia
  e) Hypoglycemia

2.23 What term refers to the replacement of normal parenchymal tissue with connective tissue?
  a) Alopecia
  b) Erythema
  c) Fibrosis
  d) Mucositis
  e) Myelosuppression

Answers on page 34

2.24 What is the medical term for a high lymphocyte count?
- a) Lymphedema
- b) Lymphocytopenia
- c) Lymphocytosis
- d) Lymphoid
- e) Lymphopoiesis

2.25 Which disease is the abnormal growth of bone, usually due to chronic kidney disease?
- a) Myelopoiesis
- b) Osteoclasis
- c) Osteodystrophy
- d) Osteoplasty
- e) Osteosis

2.26 What is the medical term for low levels of oxygen in the blood?
- a) Hematemesis
- b) Hemoptysis
- c) Hemorrhage
- d) Hypoxemia
- e) Paroxysmal

2.27 Hyperkalemia means high levels of which chemical element?
- a) Calcium
- b) Mercury
- c) Phosphorus
- d) Potassium
- e) Sodium

2.28 What is the medical term for no urine production?
- a) Anuria
- b) Diuresis
- c) Micturition
- d) Nocturia
- e) Voiding

Answers on page 35

2.29 The excision of a tissue sample for examination under a microscope is called a(n):

a) abscess

b) arthroscopy

c) biopsy

d) curettage

e) laceration

2.30 What is diastole?

a) A heart rate above 120 beats per second

b) A heart rate below 60 beats per second

c) An irregular heart rate

d) When the heart muscle contracts

e) When the heart muscle relaxes

2.31 The normal range for a test is known as the:

a) coefficient of variation

b) reference range

c) specificity

d) standard deviation

e) standard range

2.32 What is the medical term for an abnormally low urine volume?

a) Aciduria

b) Azoturia

c) Oliguria

d) Polyuria

e) Pyuria

2.33 What is the term for an elevated level of white blood cells in urine?

a) Hematuria

b) Nephritis

c) Pyelonephritis

d) Pyuria

e) Uremia

Answers on page 35

2.34 What is erythropoiesis?

   a) A red blood cell transfusion

   b) Decreased tissue demand for oxygen

   c) Hypoxia of cells that produce erythropoietin

   d) The destruction of red blood cells

   e) The process of red blood cells production

2.35 A hospitalized patient has this sign above their bed:

What does the sign mean?

   a) Do not intubate

   b) Do not resuscitate

   c) No blood draws allowed

   d) No food or drink allowed

   e) The patient is not allowed out of bed

Answers on page 35

ANSWERS

2.1 c) Increase in size

Hypertrophy refers to the increase in the size of an organ or tissue due to the enlargement of its component cells.

2.2 d) Systole

Systole is the heartbeat phase when the heart muscle contracts, pumping blood out of the heart.

2.3 d) The process by which phagocytes engulf foreign material

Phagocytosis is the process by which cells called phagocytes ingest other cells or particles.

2.4 d) Pap test

The Pap test (Papanicolaou test) is a procedure to test for cervical cancer in women.

2.5 a) glucose

Glycolysis is the breakdown of glucose into pyruvate and ATP (energy).

2.6 d) Hemopoiesis

Hemopoiesis is the process of creating new blood cells in the body. The term is from *hemo* (meaning blood) and *poiesis* (meaning production).

2.7 b) leukocytes

White blood cells are called leukocytes. The word leukocyte comes from *leuko* meaning 'white' and *cyte* meaning 'cell'.

White blood cells are the immune system cells that fight infectious diseases.

2.8 c) type of blood clot

A thrombus is a blood clot that forms in a vessel and remains there, which can restrict or block blood flow.

2.9 d) Slow

Brady- means slow. For example, bradycardia refers to a slow heart rate.

2.10 a) Glands

Adeno- refers to a gland or glands, as in adenoma (a benign tumor of a gland) and adenopathy (disease of the glands).

2.11 a) Blood condition

Words that end with -emia are blood conditions. Examples are leukemia (blood cancer), anemia (low levels of red blood cells), and uremia (the presence of urine waste products in the blood).

2.12 c) -oma

The suffix -oma means "tumor" or "mass". Examples are lymphoma (cancer of the lymphatic system) and melanoma (a type of skin cancer).

Option a, -algia, means "pain", as in myalgia and fibromyalgia.

Option b, -emia, means a blood condition.

Option d, -osis, means a disease or condition such as lymphosis or hepatosis.

Option e, -tomy, means an incision.

2.13 e) Prostate-specific antigen

PSA stands for prostate-specific antigen. It is a protein produced by the prostate gland. The PSA test measures the level of PSA in the blood. A high PSA level may indicate prostate cancer.

2.14 d) quantity not sufficient

QNS stands for quantity not sufficient, meaning the sample collected is not enough to perform the test.

2.15 b) evacuated tube

The evacuated tube system (ETS) is the standard equipment for venipuncture. It consists of a needle device, a tube holder, and an air-evacuated tube.

2.16 c) Complete blood count

A complete blood count (CBC) is a test that counts the number of red blood cells, white blood cells, and platelets in a blood sample.

2.17 e) petechiae

Petechiae are small red spots on the patient's skin caused by bleeding. For a phlebotomist, these spots may indicate that the patient has a coagulation problem and that the patient's venipuncture site may bleed excessively.

2.18 d) Swelling caused by fluid retention

Edema is swelling caused by excess fluid trapped in the body's tissues.

2.19 d) An abnormal connection between two parts of the body

A fistula is an abnormal connection between two spaces in the body. This can be blood vessels, intestines, or organs. Fistulas are usually caused by injury or surgery.

2.20 c) A localized collection of blood outside the blood vessels

A hematoma is a localized collection of blood outside a blood vessel. Hematomas are usually caused by an injured blood vessel, causing blood to seep out of the blood vessel into the surrounding tissue

2.21 d) Blood in the urine

Hematuria is blood in urine. *Hema* means "blood" and *uria* means "urine".

2.22 e) Hypoglycemia

Hypoglycemia is a low blood glucose level. The word "hypoglycemia" is derived from the Greek elements *hypo* (meaning "low") + *glyco* (meaning "sugar") + *emia* (meaning "blood").

2.23 c) Fibrosis

Fibrosis is the replacement of normal parenchymal tissue with thicker, stiffer connective tissue. It often occurs due to injury or inflammation.

2.24 c) Lymphocytosis

Lymphocytosis is the medical term for a high lymphocyte count. It is derived from the word lymphocyte and the suffix *-osis* (meaning 'abnormal' or 'increase').

2.25 c) Osteodystrophy

Osteodystrophy refers to abnormal changes in the growth and formation of bone. It is often due to renal (kidney) disease.

Myelopoiesis is the production of bone marrow and bone marrow cells.

Osteoclasis is the surgical destruction of bone.

Osteoplasty is the surgical repair of bone.

Osteosis is the formation of bone tissue.

2.26 d) Hypoxemia

Hypoxemia is the term for a below-normal level of oxygen in the blood. The word is derived from *hypo* (low) + *oxy* (oxygen) + *emia* (blood).

2.27 d) Potassium

Hyperkalemia is a condition where potassium levels in the blood are too high. Hyper means "high" and kalemia means potassium in the blood.

2.28 a) Anuria

Anuria is the absence of urine production.

2.29 c) biopsy

A biopsy is a medical procedure that involves taking a small sample of body tissue for examination under a microscope.

2.30 e) When the heart muscle relaxes

Diastole is the period between heartbeats when the heart relaxes and fills with blood.

2.31 b) reference range

The reference range is the set of values considered normal.

2.32 c) Oliguria

Oliguria is the medical term for a decreased output of urine. Oliguria is considered to be a urinary output of less than 400 millilitres over 24 hours.

2.33 d) Pyuria

Pyuria is a high level of white blood cells in urine. It is defined as 10 or more white cells per cubic millimetre in a urine specimen.

Hematuria is the presence of blood in urine.

Nephritis is inflammation of the kidneys.

Pyelonephritis is a type of urinary tract infection.

Uremia is the term for high levels of urea in blood.

2.34 e) The process of red blood cells production

Erythropoiesis is the creation of red blood cells. The word comes from *erythro* meaning "white" and *poiesis* meaning "synthesis".

2.35 d) No food or drink allowed

NPO means nil per os, which translates to "nothing by mouth". It means the patient is not allowed to eat or drink.

Competency 3

Basic Biology, Anatomy and Physiology

There are 65 questions in this competency.

3.1 What is the basic structural and functional unit of the human body?

a) Cell

b) DNA

c) Organ

d) System

e) Tissue

3.2 What is the major cation found in extracellular fluid?

a) Chloride

b) Magnesium

c) Potassium

d) Sodium

e) Zinc

Answers on page 52

3.3 Which system is a complex network of glands and organs
that uses hormones to control and coordinate metabolism,
growth, development, and mood?

a) Digestive

b) Endocrine

c) Lymphatic

d) Nervous

e) Reproductive

3.4 Oxygen and nutrients pass from the blood to the tissues
via the:

a) arteries

b) arterioles

c) capillaries

d) lymphatic vessels

e) veins

3.5 What is the sequence of hemostasis?

a) Coagulation, platelet plug formation, vasoconstriction

b) Coagulation, vasoconstriction, platelet plug formation

c) Platelet plug formation, coagulation, vasoconstriction

d) Vasoconstriction, coagulation, platelet plug formation

e) Vasoconstriction, platelet plug formation, coagulation

3.6 Night blindness is caused by a deficiency in which vitamin?

a) Vitamin A

b) Vitamin B12

c) Vitamin B6

d) Vitamin C

e) Vitamin D

3.7 Jaundice is caused by a buildup of _____ in
the blood.

a) bacteria

b) bilirubin

c) hemoglobin

d) potassium

e) uric acid

Answers on page 52

3.8 Which process involves coating pathogens with antibodies to increase their susceptibility to phagocytosis?

a) Agglutination

b) Antiperistalsis

c) Chemotaxis

d) Complement activation

e) Opsonization

3.9 Complement can be activated through three pathways: classical, lectin, and:

a) alternative

b) concurrent

c) contemporary

d) modern

e) tertiary

3.10 Which cells produce histamine in a type 1 hypersensitivity reaction?

a) Lymphocytes

b) Macrophages

c) Mast cells

d) Neutrophils

e) T cells

Answers on page 52

3.11 Which bone is the femur?

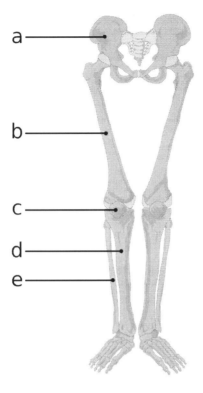

a) a
b) b
c) c
d) d
e) e

3.12 The larger of the two lower leg bones is called the:
a) condoyle
b) cranial
c) fibula
d) tibia
e) ulna

Answers on page 53

3.13 Which fibrous connective tissue connects muscle to bone?

    a) Cartilage

    b) Ligament

    c) Muscle fibre

    d) Nerve

    e) Tendon

3.14 Which hormone is also known as epinephrine?

    a) Adrenaline

    b) Cortisol

    c) Oxytocin

    d) Testosterone

    e) Vasopressin

3.15 Which gland secretes cortisol?

    a) Adrenal

    b) Pineal

    c) Pituitary

    d) Thymus

    e) Thyroid

3.16 Which gland produces growth hormone?

    a) Adrenal

    b) Endocrine

    c) Pancreas

    d) Parathyroid

    e) Pituitary

3.17 Which hormone is antagonistic to insulin?

    a) Calcitonin

    b) FSH

    c) Glucagon

    d) Thyroxine

    e) Vasopressin

Answers on page 53

3.18 The thyroid gland is located next to the:

    a) brain

    b) kidneys

    c) larynx

    d) liver

    e) spleen

3.19 Which gland produces thyroid-stimulating hormone?

    a) Adrenals

    b) Parathyroids

    c) Pituitary

    d) Testes

    e) Thyroid

3.20 What is the functional unit of the kidney?

    a) Alveoli

    b) Glomerular tuft

    c) Glomerulus

    d) Loop of Henle

    e) Nephron

3.21 In the kidneys, substances travel from the glomerulus into the Bowman capsule by which process?

    a) Active transport

    b) Diffusion

    c) Evaporation

    d) Filtration

    e) Osmosis

3.22 What are the end products of protein digestion?

    a) Amino acids

    b) Enzymes

    c) Fatty acids

    d) Monosaccharides

    e) Triglycerides

Answers on page 53

3.23 The end products of fat digestion are fatty acids and:
   a) alkaloids
   b) amino acids
   c) glucose
   d) glycerol
   e) sebum

3.24 After leaving the stomach, food next enters the:
   a) esophagus
   b) large intestine
   c) liver
   d) rectum
   e) small intestine

3.25 The small intestine consists of the duodenum, jejunum and:
   a) anal canal
   b) cecum
   c) colon
   d) ileum
   e) rectum

3.26 Nerve cells are also called:
   a) axons
   b) dendrites
   c) glial cells
   d) neuroglial cells
   e) neurons

3.27 Which part of a neuron carries impulses away from the neuron?
   a) Axon
   b) Cell body
   c) Dendrite
   d) Myelin sheath
   e) Schwann cell

Answers on page 54

3.28 The central nervous system includes the:
   a) brain and spinal cord
   b) heart
   c) peripheral nerves
   d) somatic nerves
   e) spinal nerves

3.29 The impulse in a neuron moves from the
_____ to the _____ .
   a) Schwann cell, myelin
   b) axon, dendrite
   c) cell body, myelin
   d) dendrite, axon
   e) myelin, Schwann cell

3.30 What are the smallest blood vessels in the body?
   a) Arteries
   b) Capillaries
   c) Lymph nodes
   d) Lymph vessels
   e) Veins

3.31 Which part of the heart sets the heart rate?
   a) AV node
   b) Left atrium
   c) Right atrium
   d) Sinoatrial node
   e) VA node

3.32 On which part of the body is the basilic vein?
   a) Arm
   b) Foot
   c) Hand
   d) Leg
   e) Neck

Answers on page 54

3.33 Which is the largest artery in the body?

   a) Aorta

   b) Carotid artery

   c) Iliac artery

   d) Pulmonary artery

   e) Superior vena cava

3.34 Refer to the image below:

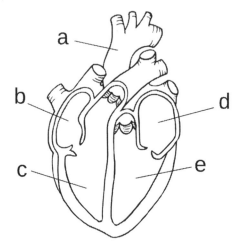

Which line is pointing to the left atrium?

   a) a

   b) b

   c) c

   d) d

   e) e

3.35 From the left atrium, blood next flows into the:

   a) aorta

   b) left lung

   c) left ventricle

   d) right atrium

   e) right ventricle

Answers on page 54

3.36 Which of these is a vein in the arm?
   a) Femoral
   b) Jugular
   c) Median cubital
   d) Portal
   e) Radial

3.37 Which skin structure helps prevent water loss and inhibits bacterial growth on the surface of the skin?
   a) Arrector pili
   b) Hair follicles
   c) Nerves
   d) Oil glands
   e) Sweat glands

3.38 The dermis is:
   a) above the epidermis
   b) also known as subcutaneous tissue
   c) also known as the epithelial layer
   d) the basal layer of the skin
   e) the middle layer of the skin

3.39 In which organelle does ATP production occur?
   a) Flagellum
   b) Golgi apparatus
   c) Mitochondrion
   d) Nucleus
   e) Rough endoplasmic reticulum

3.40 Which cellular component is involved in packaging enzymes?
   a) Centrioles
   b) Endoplasmic reticulum
   c) Golgi apparatus
   d) Mitochondria
   e) Ribosomes

Answers on page 55

3.41 What are the three major disaccharides?

    a) Glucose, galactose, and fructose

    b) Glucose, galactose, and lactose

    c) Glucose, lactose, and sucrose

    d) Lactose, fructose, and galactose

    e) Sucrose, lactose, and maltose

3.42 What is the main detoxification organ?

    a) Adenoids

    b) Kidneys

    c) Liver

    d) Pancreas

    e) Spleen

3.43 Which organ is the line pointing to?

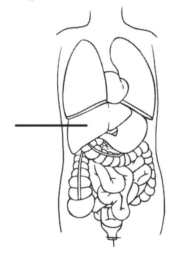

    a) Bladder

    b) Gallbladder

    c) Liver

    d) Pancreas

    e) Stomach

Answers on page 55

3.44 Which enzyme unwinds DNA?
   a) Helicase
   b) Hexonuclease
   c) Ligase
   d) Primase
   e) Topoisomerase

3.45 DNA polymerase can synthesize:
   a) DNA in the 3' to 5' direction
   b) DNA in the 5' to 3' direction
   c) RNA in the 3' to 5' direction
   d) RNA in the 5' to 3' direction
   e) mRNA in the 3' to 5' direction

3.46 How many nucleotides are in a codon?
   a) 1
   b) 2
   c) 3
   d) 4
   e) 5

3.47 In DNA, which base pairs with cytosine?
   a) Cytosine
   b) Guanine
   c) Thymine
   d) Uracil
   e) Xanthine

3.48 Antibody class is determined by the:
   a) constant region of the heavy chain
   b) constant region of the light chain
   c) disulphide bonds
   d) variable region of the heavy chain
   e) variable region of the light chain

Answers on page 55

3.49 High levels of which lipoprotein are associated with a
decreased risk of accelerated atherosclerosis?

    a) Chylomicrons

    b) HDL

    c) Insulin

    d) LDL

    e) VLDL

3.50 The simplest form of carbohydrate is called a:

    a) free fatty acid

    b) glycerol molecule

    c) monosaccharide

    d) nucleotide

    e) protein

3.51 Lactose is a disaccharide of which two monosaccharides?

    a) Fructose and galactose

    b) Glucose and fructose

    c) Glucose and galactose

    d) Glucose and glucose

    e) Glucose and xylose

3.52 Which organ does hydrogen breath testing investigate?

    a) Bladder

    b) Intestine

    c) Liver

    d) Lungs

    e) Stomach

3.53 Which blood cells defend the body against disease?

    a) Erythrocytes

    b) Hematocytes

    c) Leukocytes

    d) Osteocytes

    e) Thrombocytes

Answers on page 56

3.54 Which component of blood carries oxygen?

   a) Antigens

   b) Granulocytes

   c) Hemoglobin

   d) Platelets

   e) White blood cells

3.55 What is this blood cell?

   a) B cell

   b) Macrophage

   c) Neutrophil

   d) Platelet

   e) Red blood cell

3.56 Hematopoiesis occurs mainly in the:

   a) blood

   b) bone marrow

   c) brain

   d) liver

   e) pancreas

3.57 A reticulocyte is:

   a) a mature red blood cell

   b) an immature erythrocyte

   c) demonstrated using a Wright-Giemsa stain

   d) found only in the bone marrow

   e) part of the reticuloendothelial system

Answers on page 56

3.58 Phagocytes:

    a) carry carbon dioxide around the body

    b) carry oxygen around the body

    c) form clots to stop bleeding

    d) ingest pathogens

    e) release antibodies against pathogens

3.59 Which of these white blood cells is a phagocyte?

    a) B cell

    b) Basophil

    c) Eosinophil

    d) Neutrophil

    e) T cell

3.60 What are the two main types of lymphocytes?

    a) B cells and T cells

    b) Cytotoxic cells and helper cells

    c) Granulocytes and agranulocytes

    d) Macrophages and thrombocytes

    e) Plasma cells and memory cells

3.61 Which of these cells is a granulocyte?

    a) Dendritic cell

    b) Macrophage

    c) Natural killer T cell

    d) Natural killer cell

    e) Neutrophil

3.62 The three types of granulocyte are neutrophils, eosinophils, and:

    a) basophils

    b) erythrocytes

    c) lymphocytes

    d) monocytes

    e) thrombocytes

Answers on page 57

3.63 Which blood cell is typically the first to appear in the response to an infection?

a) Basophil

b) Eosinophil

c) Eosinophil

d) Erythrocyte

e) Neutrophil

3.64 Which test can diagnose HIV in the early stages of infection, before antibodies are detectable?

a) Immunelectrophoresis

b) Nucleic acid test (NAT)

c) Ouchterlony double diffusion

d) Radioimmunoassay (RIA)

e) The Quellung test

3.65 Which test detects antibodies attached to red blood cells?

a) Antibody screen

b) Direct antiglobulin test

c) Elution

d) Indirect antiglobulin test

e) Radioallergosorbent (RAST) test

Answers on page 57

ANSWERS

3.1 a) Cell

Cells are the basic structural and functional unit of the body. They are the "building blocks" of larger structures like tissues and organs.

3.2 d) Sodium

In extracellular fluid, the major cation is sodium and the major anion is chloride.

3.3 b) Endocrine

The endocrine system, also called the hormonal system, consists of glands and organs that produce hormones. These hormones regulate various body functions, including metabolism, growth, and mood.

3.4 c) capillaries

Capillaries are the smallest blood vessels in the body, and their thin walls allow oxygen and nutrients to pass from the blood to the tissues. They also allow waste products to pass from tissues into the blood for removal.

3.5 e) Vasoconstriction, platelet plug formation, coagulation

Hemostasis is the process that stops bleeding after an injury. It involves three steps:

1. Vasoconstriction: Constriction of blood vessels to reduce blood flow to the area and minimize blood loss.
2. Platelet plug formation: Temporary blockage of the hole by a platelet plug.
3. Coagulation: Formation of a stable blood clot to firmly seal the wound.

3.6 a) Vitamin A

Vitamin A is essential for normal vision. A deficiency can lead to visual problems such as night blindness (difficulty seeing in dim light or darkness) and xerophthalmia (dryness of the eye's surface).

3.7 b) bilirubin

Jaundice is when the body turns yellow due to too much bilirubin in the blood. Bilirubin is a yellow pigment produced during the breakdown of red blood cells.

3.8 e) Opsonization

Opsonization is a process where opsonins (e.g., antibodies) coat pathogens so phagocytes can recognise and ingest them.

3.9 a) alternative

The complement system enhances the ability of the immune system to clear microbes and damaged cells. It can be activated through three pathways: the classical pathway (triggered by antibodies), the lectin pathway (triggered by lectins binding to pathogens), and the alternative pathway (spontaneous activation on pathogen surfaces).

3.10 c) Mast cells

Type I hypersensitivities include asthma, rhinitis, and food allergies. In this type of hypersensitivity, mast cells release large amounts of histamine and other inflammatory mediators.

3.11 b) b

The femur is the thigh bone.

3.12 d) tibia

The two lower leg bones are the tibia and fibula. Both bones run from the knee to the ankle, but the tibia is thicker and slightly longer.

3.13 e) Tendon

Tendons connect muscle to bone.

Cartilage is a tissue that protects the ends of bones at the joints.

Ligaments connect bone to bone.

Muscle fibre is what muscles are made up of.

3.14 a) Adrenaline

Epinephrine, also known as adrenaline, is a hormone produced by the adrenal glands. It plays a key role in the body's fight-or-flight response by increasing heart rate, blood flow, and energy supply.

3.15 a) Adrenal

The adrenal glands are on top of the kidneys and make hormones including cortisol, aldosterone, and adrenaline.

3.16 e) Pituitary

The pituitary gland produces several hormones, including growth hormone, adrenocorticotropic hormone (ACTH), follicle-stimulating hormone, luteinizing hormone, prolactin, thyroid-stimulating hormone, vasopressin, and oxytocin.

Growth hormone stimulates growth in children and teenagers. In adults, it stimulates muscle formation and reduces fat tissue.

3.17 c) Glucagon

Insulin lowers the concentration of glucose in the blood. Glucagon has the opposite effect by increasing the glucose concentration in the blood.

3.18 c) larynx

The thyroid gland is located at the front of the neck just below the Adam's apple (larynx).

3.19 c) Pituitary

The pituitary gland produces thyroid-stimulating hormone (TSH). TSH stimulates the thyroid gland to produce T3 and T4.

3.20 e) Nephron

The functional unit of the kidney is the nephron. Nephrons are responsible for removing waste from the body. Each kidney has over a million nephrons.

Option a, alveoli, is the functional unit of the lungs.

The glomerular tuft, glomerulus, and loop of Henle are all structures inside nephrons. They are not the kidney's functional unit.

3.21 d) Filtration

During filtration, substances that are small enough, like water, electrolytes, glucose, and waste products, pass through the filtration barrier and into the Bowman capsule. Larger molecules, like blood cells and proteins, are too big and remain in the bloodstream.

3.22 a) Amino acids

Proteins are made of amino acids Enzymes called proteases break proteins down into smaller proteins or amino acids.

3.23 d) glycerol

A fat molecule consists of fatty acids and glycerol.

3.24 e) small intestine

After food is processed in the stomach, it moves into the small intestine, where most of the digestion and absorption of nutrients occurs. The small intestine is divided into three parts: the duodenum, jejunum, and ileum. After the small intestine, waste moves into the large intestine, and finally leaves the body as feces.

3.25 d) ileum

The small intestine consists of the duodenum, jejunum, and ileum. The large intestine consists of the cecum, colon, rectum, and anal canal.

3.26 e) neurons

Nerve cells are also called neurons. They are the main cells of the nervous system. They consist of a cell body, an axon (which sends signals), and dendrites (which receive signals).

3.27 a) Axon

The axon is a thin extension of a neuron that transmits electrical signals away from the cell body, typically to other neurons.

3.28 a) brain and spinal cord

The central nervous system (CNS) consists of the brain and spinal cord. It processes information and coordinates all activities of the body.

The peripheral nervous system (PNS) consists of the nerves that branch out from the brain and spinal cord and extend to other parts of the body, such as the muscles and organs.

3.29 d) dendrite, axon

The impulse in a neuron travels from the dendrites, which receive the signal, through the cell body, and down the axon to the axon terminals, where it is transmitted to a muscle cell or another neuron.

3.30 b) Capillaries

Capillaries are the smallest blood vessels in the body.

3.31 d) Sinoatrial node

The sinoatrial (SA) node is known as the heart's pacemaker because it regulates the heart rate.

3.32 a) Arm

The basilic vein is a vein of the arm and is sometimes used for phlebotomy.

3.33 a) Aorta

The largest artery is the aorta. It carries blood from the heart to the rest of the body.

3.34 d) d

On diagrams of the heart, the left atrium is in the upper-right corner.

3.35 c) left ventricle

From the left atrium, blood next flows into the left ventricle. The left ventricle then pumps the oxygenated blood into the aorta, distributing it to the body.

3.36 c) Median cubital

The median cubital vein is a prominent arm vein commonly used for venipuncture. It is located in the antecubital fossa, the area in front of the elbow.

3.37 d) Oil glands

Oil glands secrete sebum, an oily substance that helps prevent water loss and inhibits bacterial growth on the skin surface.

3.38 e) the middle layer of the skin

The dermis is the middle layer of the skin. It is located under the epidermis and above the subcutaneous tissue.

3.39 c) Mitochondrion

The mitochondrion is known as the powerhouse of the cell because it produces ATP (adenosine triphosphate), the cell's energy source.

3.40 c) Golgi apparatus

In human cells, the Golgi apparatus modifies, sorts, and packages proteins and enzymes for secretion or use.

3.41 e) Sucrose, lactose, and maltose

Disaccharides are sugars formed by two monosaccharides joined together. Three common examples are sucrose, lactose, and maltose.

3.42 c) Liver

Detoxification is mainly carried out by the liver. It processes toxins and various metabolic wastes so that they can be excreted through the kidneys (via urine) or the gut (via feces).

3.43 c) Liver

The liver is under the lungs, in the upper right area of the abdomen.

3.44 a) Helicase

Helicase enzymes move along the DNA and separate the strands.

3.45 b) DNA in the 5' to 3' direction

DNA polymerase synthesizes new strands of DNA. It does this in the 5' to 3' direction.

3.46 c) 3

A codon is a sequence of three nucleotides in DNA or RNA. Each codon codes for a specific amino acid. For example, the nucleotides UUU code for the amino acid phenylalanine, and CUU codes for leucine.

3.47 b) Guanine

In DNA, cytosine pairs with guanine (C-G) and adenine pairs with thymine (A-T).

3.48 a) constant region of the heavy chain

An antibody's class is determined by the constant region of its heavy chain. This region creates the Fc region, which is vital for binding to Fc receptors on other cell types and mediating antibody functions.

3.49 b) HDL

High-density lipoprotein (HDL) decreases the risk of atherosclerosis and is known as the "good" cholesterol.

In contrast, low-density lipoprotein (LDL), very-low-density lipoprotein (VLDL), and chylomicrons increase the risk of atherosclerosis.

Insulin is a peptide hormone, not a lipoprotein.

3.50 c) monosaccharide

Monosaccharides are the simplest form of carbohydrates. They include glucose, fructose, and galactose. They are the building blocks of more complex carbohydrates.

3.51 c) Glucose and galactose

Lactose is a disaccharide composed of one glucose molecule and one galactose molecule.

The disaccharide composed of one glucose molecule and one fructose molecule is sucrose.

The disaccharide composed of two glucose molecules is maltose.

3.52 b) Intestine

Hydrogen breath testing detects diseases of the small intestine. These diseases are:

1. bacterial overgrowth of the small intestine
2. carbohydrate malabsorption (e.g. lactose, fructose, or sucrose intolerance)
3. the rapid or slow passage of food through the small intestine

The test measures the amount of hydrogen in the breath after the patient drinks a liquid containing a specific amount of sugar.

3.53 c) Leukocytes

Leukocytes (also known as white blood cells) are the cells that protect the body from disease.

Option a, erythrocytes, are red blood cells (cells that carry oxygen and carbon dioxide around the body).

Option b, hematocytes, is a term for any kind of blood cell.

Option d, osteocytes, are bone cells.

Option e, thrombocytes, are platelets (cells that help with clotting).

3.54 c) Hemoglobin

Hemoglobin is a protein in red blood cells that carries oxygen. Hemoglobin

can also carry carbon dioxide, a waste product of cellular respiration.

3.55 d) Platelet

The image shows a platelet. Normally platelets have a smooth surface, but they grow spike-like pseudopods when activated upon blood vessel damage. These pseudopods can be seen in the image – they are the spike-like projections growing out of the cell. These "spikes" allow the platelets to grip to one another and to stringy chains of proteins called fibrin, forming clots.

3.56 b) bone marrow

Hematopoiesis is the creation of new blood cells. In adults, hematopoiesis occurs mainly in the bone marrow.

3.57 b) an immature erythrocyte

A reticulocyte is an immature red blood cell recently released from the bone marrow into the bloodstream. It matures into an erythrocyte within a day or two.

3.58 d) ingest pathogens

Phagocytes are cells that ingest harmful particles, bacteria, and dead cells. Their name comes from phago, meaning "to eat", and cyte, meaning "cell".

3.59 d) Neutrophil

Phagocytes are a type of white blood cell specialized in ingesting and destroying pathogens. Monocytes, macrophages, neutrophils, and dendritic cells are phagocytes.

In contrast, white blood cells that do not function as phagocytes include basophils, eosinophils, and lymphocytes (B cells, T cells, and natural killer cells).

3.60 a) B cells and T cells

Lymphocytes are a type of immune cell. The two main types of lymphocytes are B cells and T cells.

B cells make antibodies. T cells help kill tumor cells and control immune responses.

Cytotoxic cells and helper cells are different functions of T cells.

3.61 e) Neutrophil

The three types of granulocyte are neutrophils, eosinophils and basophils.

Dendritic cell and macrophage are incorrect because they have no granules in their cytoplasms.

Although natural killer cells and natural killer T cells have granules, these cells are large granular lymphocytes, not granulocytes.

3.62 a) basophils

Granulocytes are white blood cells that release granules during infections, allergic reactions, and asthma. The three types of granulocyte are neutrophils, eosinophils, and basophils.

3.63 e) Neutrophil

The first blood cells to appear during an infection are usually neutrophils. Neutrophils are released into the bloodstream in large numbers in response to an infection. They are white blood cells that kill and digest bacteria.

3.64 b) Nucleic acid test (NAT)

The nucleic acid test (NAT) directly detects the presence of the human immunodeficiency virus (HIV) by identifying its RNA. Out of all HIV tests, the nucleic acid test can detect HIV the soonest (about 10 to 33 days after exposure).

3.65 b) Direct antiglobulin test

The direct antiglobulin test detects antibodies attached to red blood cells.

The indirect antiglobulin test detects antibodies present in the bloodstream.

Competency 4

Laboratory Mathematics and Quality Management

There are 45 questions in this competency.

4.1 A molar solution is:
   a) 1 mL of solute in 1 litre of solution
   b) 1 mL of solute in one mole of solution
   c) one gram of solute in 1 mL of solution
   d) one gram of solute in one mole of solution
   e) one mole of solute in 1 litre of solution

4.2 What is the dilution factor 1/5 expressed as a dilution ratio?
   a) 1:4
   b) 1:5
   c) 1:6
   d) 5:1
   e) 5:4

Answers on page 69

4.3 A lab technician is making a solution by combining 3 parts of a solute with 7 parts of water. How many millilitres of the solute and water are needed to make 100 mL of the solution?

   a) 7 mL of solute and 3 mL of water
   b) 10 mL of solute and 70 mL of water
   c) 30 mL of solute and 70 mL of water
   d) 70 mL of solute and 30 mL of water
   e) 300 mL of solute and 700 mL of water

4.4 If a dilution ratio of 7:10 is used to make an acetic acid solution and the final volume of the solution is 950 mL, what is the volume of the solute?

   a) 58 mL
   b) 101 mL
   c) 391 mL
   d) 559 mL
   e) 665 mL

4.5 A lab technician adds 0.2 mL of a stock solution to 3.8 mL of diluent. What is the dilution factor?

   a) 4
   b) 5
   c) 19
   d) 20
   e) 21

4.6 0.5 mol of solute is dissolved in 250 cm^3 of solution. What is the concentration in mol/dm^3?

   a) 0.002 mol/dm^3
   b) 2 mol/dm^3
   c) 12.5 mol/dm^3
   d) 125 mol/dm^3
   e) 500 mol/dm^3

Answers on page 69

4.7 What does the unit mol/kg represent?

a) Milli-molarity

b) Molality

c) Molar concentration

d) Molar mass

e) Molarity

4.8 How many grams of sodium chloride are needed to make 200 mL of a 5% m/v sodium chloride solution?

a) 5 g

b) 10 g

c) 15 g

d) 20 g

e) 25 g

4.9 How do you calculate the mass of a solute in a solution?

a) Concentration / volume

b) Concentration $\times$ volume

c) Volume + concentration

d) Volume – concentration

e) Volume/concentration

4.10 A lab technician requires 400 mL of a 3% solution but has only a 5% solution available. How would the lab technician prepare the 3% solution?

a) Mix 240 mL of the 5% solution with 160 mL of diluent

b) Mix 300 mL of the 5% solution with 100 mL of diluent

c) Mix 360 mL of the 5% solution with 40 mL of diluent

d) Mix 380 mL of the 5% solution with 20 mL of diluent

e) Mix 388 mL of the 5% solution with 12 mL of diluent

4.11 How many millilitres of an 80% acetic acid solution is needed to make 2 litres of a 10% acetic acid solution?

a) 20

b) 50

c) 100

d) 250

e) 500

Answers on page 70

4.12 How would you prepare 400 mL of a 1% v/v acetic acid
solution?

    a) 1 mL of glacial acetic acid in 399 mL of water

    b) 2 mL of glacial acetic acid in 398 mL of water

    c) 3 mL of glacial acetic acid in 397 mL of water

    d) 4 mL of glacial acetic acid in 396 mL of water

    e) 40 mL of glacial acetic acid in 400 mL of water

4.13 What does 5% w/v mean?

    a) 5 grams of solute dissolved in 100 mL of solution

    b) 5 grams of solute dissolved in 100 mL of solvent

    c) 5 grams of solution dissolved in 95 mL of solution

    d) 5 mL of solute dissolved in 100 mL of solution

    e) 5 mL of solute dissolved in 100 mL of solvent

4.14 Calculate the %m/m of a solution that has 30 grams of
solute and 90 grams of solvent.

    a) 8.3%

    b) 9.1%

    c) 11%

    d) 25%

    e) 31%

4.15 Which of these expresses solution concentration for a solid
solute dissolved in a liquid solvent?

    a) %(m/m)

    b) %(m/v)

    c) %(v/m)

    d) %(v/v)

    e) %(w/m)

4.16 What is the formula for calculating a percent w/w
solution?

    a) (solute mass / solution mass) × 100

    b) (solute mass / solution volume) × 100

    c) (solution mass / solute mass) × 100

    d) (solution mass / solute volume) × 100

    e) (solution volume / solute volume) × 100

Answers on page 71

4.17 A mg is a unit to describe:

    a) length

    b) mass

    c) speed

    d) time

    e) volume

4.18 Which prefix means 10^{-6}?

    a) Centi-

    b) Kilo-

    c) Micro-

    d) Milli-

    e) Nano-

4.19 What does the prefix kilo- mean?

    a) 10

    b) 100

    c) 1,000

    d) 10,000

    e) 100,000

4.20 Which prefix means 0.001?

    a) Micro-

    b) Centi-

    c) Pico-

    d) Milli-

    e) Nano-

4.21 What is 40°F in Celsius and rounded to the nearest whole number?

    a) −19°C

    b) 4°C

    c) 21°C

    d) 37°C

    e) 52°C

Answers on page 72

4.22 What is 100°C in Fahrenheit?

a) 45°F

b) 78°F

c) 157°F

d) 212°F

e) 274°F

4.23 Round 2.08691 to three decimal places.

a) 2.08

b) 2.086

c) 2.087

d) 2.089

e) 2.09

4.24 What is 89.9583 rounded to three significant figures?

a) 89.8

b) 89.9

c) 89.958

d) 90.0

e) 91.0

4.25 What is 1 dm^3 in cm^3?

a) 0.001 cm^3

b) 0.01 cm^3

c) 0.1 cm^3

d) 10 cm^3

e) 1,000 cm^3

4.26 What is 0.05 mL in microlitres?

a) 0.00005 μ L

b) 0.0005 μ L

c) 0.005 μ L

d) 5 μ L

e) 50 μ L

Answers on page 72

4.27 The chart below shows a patient's blood carbon dioxide
levels over one week.

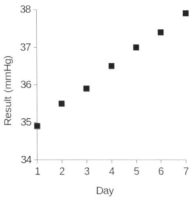

What type of trend does the chart demonstrate?

a) Exponential

b) Linear

c) Logarithmic

d) Polynomial

e) Power

4.28 For data distributed normally, how many values are within
two standard deviations from the mean?

a) 50%

b) 68%

c) 83%

d) 95%

e) 99.7%

Answers on page 72

4.29 The following data were calculated on a series of 100 determinations of a control.

Mean	5.8
Median	6.0
Mode	5.7
Range	1.5–20.2
Standard deviation	0.25

If confidence limits are set at ± 2 standard deviations, what are the allowable limits for the control?

a) 5.30–6.30
b) 5.35–6.25
c) 5.50–5.90
d) 5.60–5.90
e) 5.65–5.95

4.30 A test has a mean of 72 mmol/L and a standard deviation of 3 mmol/L. If all control values must fall within 3 standard deviations of the mean, which of the following values is outside the acceptable range?

a) 62 mmol/L
b) 71 mmol/L
c) 78 mmol/L
d) 80 mmol/L
e) 81 mmol/L

4.31 A hospital wants to set a new reference range for fasting blood glucose. It measures the fasting blood glucose levels of 451 healthy patients. The mean is 4.7 mmol/L and the standard deviation is 0.4 mmol/L. Calculate a reference range that covers 95% of the patients.

a) 0.4–4.7 mmol/L
b) 3.7–5.7 mmol/L
c) 3.9–5.5 mmol/L
d) 4.3–5.1 mmol/L
e) 4.3–5.7 mmol/L

Answers on page 73

4.32 Which formula calculates the coefficient of variation?
   a) Mean / standard deviation
   b) Mean / variance
   c) Standard deviation / mean
   d) Standard deviation / variance
   e) Variance / mean

4.33 Automated white blood cell counts were performed on 29 blood samples. The mean value was 8.0 cells/nL and the standard deviation was 1.2 cells/nL. What is the coefficient of variation?
   a) 15%
   b) 30%
   c) 45%
   d) 60%
   e) 75%

4.34 What is the mean of the values 2, 2, 5, 7, and 14?
   a) 2
   b) 3
   c) 4
   d) 5
   e) 6

4.35 The middle value in a sorted data set is called the:
   a) average
   b) coefficient of variation
   c) mean
   d) median
   e) mode

4.36 If you add up all the values in a set and then divide the total by the number of values, you get the:
   a) coefficient of variation
   b) mean
   c) median
   d) mode
   e) standard deviation

Answers on page 74

4.37 Tube A contains 24 mL of blood. Tube B contains 20 mL of blood. This means tube A contains _____% more blood than tube B.

a) 4
b) 16
c) 20
d) 25
e) 32

4.38 Which grade of chemical is the highest purity?

a) Commercial
b) Laboratory
c) Purified
d) Reagent
e) Technical

4.39 Which of these is a post-analytical error?

a) A hemolyzed specimen
b) A test performed on the wrong patient
c) An empty collection tube
d) Incorrect information on the test request
e) Results reported in the wrong units

4.40 Which ISO standard specifies requirements for quality and competence in medical laboratories?

a) ISO 15106
b) ISO 15189
c) ISO 15503
d) ISO 15513
e) ISO 15520

4.41 Which of these is a pre-analytical quality indicator?

a) Critical value reporting time
b) Number of improperly labelled samples
c) Number of laboratory reporting errors
d) Percentage of results delivered late
e) Turnaround time

Answers on page 74

4.42 Which of the following is an example of a quality assurance indicator?

  a) C-reactive protein test

  b) Emergency procedures

  c) Keep thorough records of exposure incidents

  d) Laboratory staff must work under a fume hood when dealing with toxic chemicals

  e) Laboratory turnaround time

4.43 Precision indicates the:

  a) closeness of a result to the first standard deviation

  b) closeness of a result to the median value

  c) closeness of a result to the mode

  d) closeness of a result to the true value

  e) repeatability or reproducibility of a procedure

4.44 A new method for diagnosing fibromyalgia is trialled on 1,000 patients. The method detects 125 true positives, 25 false positives, 800 true negatives and 50 false negatives. Calculate the diagnostic specificity of the test.

  a) 91.9%

  b) 97.0%

  c) 98.2%

  d) 98.9%

  e) 99.3%

4.45 A test correctly identifies 50% of sick people as sick and 100% of healthy people as healthy. The test shows:

  a) bias

  b) correlation

  c) deviation

  d) sensitivity

  e) specificity

Answers on page 75

ANSWERS

4.1 e) one mole of solute in 1 litre of solution

A molar solution, often denoted as "M", is a solution that contains one mole of solute dissolved in a sufficient amount of solvent to make one litre of the solution.

4.2 a) 1:4

The dilution ratio 1:4 and the dilution factor 1/5 are different ways of expressing the same thing.

The dilution ratio 1:4 means a ratio of 1 part solute to 4 parts solvent.

The dilution factor 1/5 means the final volume of the solution is 5 times the volume of the solute. Adding 4 parts of solvent to 1 part of solute creates a 1/5 dilution.

Therefore, a 1/5 dilution factor and a 1:4 dilution ratio both create a solution with 1 part solute to 4 parts solvent.

4.3 c) 30 mL of solute and 70 mL of water

3 + 7 is a total of 10 parts.

Therefore, the amount of solute needed:

$$100 \text{ mL} \times \frac{3}{10} = 30 \text{ mL}$$

Amount of water needed:

$$100 \text{ mL} \times \frac{7}{10} = 70 \text{ mL}$$

4.4 c) 391 mL

A dilution ratio of 7:10 means the solution contains 7 parts solute and 10 parts solvent, making 17 parts in total.

In other words, 7/17ths of the solution is solute.

To find the volume of solute in a solution, multiply the volume of the solution by the fraction of the solution that is solute:

$$950 \text{ mL} \times \frac{7}{17} = 391 \text{ mL of solute}$$

4.5 d) 20

To solve this question, we must use the dilution factor formula:

$$\text{dilution factor} = \frac{\text{final volume}}{\text{initial volume}}$$

We know the initial volume is 0.2 mL but not the final volume. We can calculate the final volume by adding the initial volume of solution to the volume of the diluent:

$$0.2 \text{ mL} + 3.8 \text{ mL} = 4.0 \text{ mL}$$

Now we know the final volume, we can enter the values into the formula to calculate the dilution factor:

$$\text{dilution factor} = \frac{\text{final volume}}{\text{initial volume}}$$

$$= \frac{4.0}{0.2}$$

$$= 20$$

4.6 b) 2 mol/dm^3

First, we need to convert cm^3 to dm^3. Since one dm^3 is a thousand times larger than one cm^3, we need to divide the number of cm^3 by 1,000:

$$\frac{250}{1,000} = 0.25 \text{ dm}^3$$

Now we can work out the concentration. The concentration formula is:

$$\text{concentration} = \frac{\text{amount of solute}}{\text{volume}}$$

Inserting the values into the formula gives:

$$\text{concentration} = \frac{0.5}{0.25} = 2 \text{ mol/dm}^3$$

4.7 b) Molality

Molality is the number of moles of solute per kg of solvent. Its unit is mol/kg.

Milli-molarity is the number of milli-moles of solute in one liter of solution. Its unit is mmol/L or mM.

The molar concentration is the same as molarity. Its unit is mol/L.

Molar mass is the mass of one mole of a substance. The unit is g/mol.

Molarity is the number of moles of solute per liter of solution. The unit for molarity is mol/L or M.

4.8 b) 10 g

To find the grams of solute dissolved in a solution, multiply the solute concentration by the solution volume:

$$\text{Mass} = \text{concentration} \times \text{volume}$$

$$= 5\% \times 200 \text{ mL}$$

$$= 0.05 \times 200$$

$$= 10 \text{ g}$$

4.9 b) Concentration × volume

The formula for calculating concentration is:

$$\text{concentration} = \frac{\text{solute mass}}{\text{solution volume}}$$

This can be rearranged as:

$$\text{solute mass} = \text{concentration} \times \text{volume}$$

4.10 a) Mix 240 mL of the 5% solution with 160 mL of diluent

The dilution formula is

$$c1 \times v1 = c2 \times v2$$

where:
c1 is the initial concentration
v1 is the initial volume
c2 is the final concentration
v2 is the final volume

Using the dilution formula:

$$c1 \times v1 = c2 \times v2$$

$$5 \times v1 = 3 \times 400$$

$$5 \times v1 = 1200$$

$$v1 = \frac{1200}{5}$$

$$v1 = 240 \text{ mL}$$

Therefore, 240 mL of the 5% solution is needed.

The amount of diluent needed:

$$400 \text{ mL} - 240 \text{ mL} = 160 \text{ mL}$$

4.11 d) 250

Using the dilution formula:

$$c1 \times v1 = c2 \times v2$$

$$80 \times v1 = 2000 \times 10$$

$$80 \times v1 = 20,000$$

$$v1 = \frac{20,000}{80}$$

$$v1 = 250 \text{ mL}$$

4.12 d) 4 mL of glacial acetic acid in 396 mL of water

1% v/v means there is 1 mL of solute for every 99 mL of solvent.

To make 400 mL of 1% v/v acetic acid solution, you would take 4 mL (1% of 400 mL) of glacial acetic acid and then build it up to 400 ml by adding 396 mL of water.

4.13 a) 5 grams of solute dissolved in 100 mL of solution

w/v stands for weight/volume. It is used for solid solutes dissolved in liquid solvents.

- Weight refers to the weight of the solute and is measured in grams.
- Volume refers to the final volume of the solution and is measured in mL.

Therefore, 5% w/v means 5 g of solute for every 100 mL of solution.

4.14 d) 25%

The formula for calculating the %(m/m) of a solution is:

$$\%(m/m) = \frac{\text{solute mass}}{\text{solution mass}} \times 100$$

We know the solute mass is 30 g and the solvent mass is 90 g. However, the question does not tell us the mass of the solution.

To find the mass of the solution, add the solute and solvent mass together:

$$30 \text{ g} + 90 \text{ g} = 120 \text{ g of solution}$$

Inserting the values from the question

into the formula:

$$\%(m/m) = \frac{30}{120} \times 100$$
$$= 0.25 \times 100$$
$$= 25\%$$

4.15 b) %(m/v)

When the solute is a solid and the solvent is a liquid, a convenient way to express the concentration is as mass/volume percent. A shorter way to write this is %(m/v).

4.16 a) (solute mass / solution mass) × 100

w/w stands for weight/weight, referring to the mass (weight) of the solute and the final mass of the solution.

4.17 b) mass

mg is an abbreviation for milligram, and milligrams are a unit of mass.

4.18 c) Micro-

The prefix micro- means 10^{-6} (0.000001). Examples are the micrometre (10^{-6} metres) and the microlitre (10^{-6} litres).

The prefix centi- means a hundredth (0.01).

The prefix kilo- means a thousand (1,000).

The prefix milli- means a thousandth (0.001).

The prefix nano- means a billionth (0.000000001).

4.19 c) 1,000

The prefix kilo- means a thousand. For example, a thousand grams is called a kilogram.

4.20 d) Milli-

Milli- means one-thousandth (0.001). For example, a millimetre is one-thousandth of a metre.

4.21 b) 4°C

$$Celsius = (Fahrenheit - 32) \times \frac{5}{9}$$

$$= (40 - 32) \times \frac{5}{9}$$

$$= 8 \times \frac{5}{9}$$

$$= 4.444...$$

$$= 4°C$$

4.22 d) 212°F

$$Fahrenheit = (Celsius \times \frac{9}{5}) + 32$$

$$= 180 + 32$$

$$= 212°F$$

4.23 c) 2.087

To round 2.08691 to three decimal places, look at the fourth decimal place. The fourth fourth decimal place is 9. Since 9 is greater than 5, round the third decimal place up from 6 to 7, resulting in 2.087.

4.24 d) 90.0

The first three significant figures of 89.958 are 89.9. The next figure is a 5 which means we then need to round 89.9 up to 90.0.

89.958 is the wrong answer because this is 89.9583 rounded to three decimal places, not three significant figures.

4.25 e) 1,000 cm³

To convert from decimetres cubed to centimetres cubed, multiply the number of decimetres cubed by 1,000.

$$1 \ dm^3 \times 1,000 = 1,000 \ cm^3$$

4.26 e) 50 μ L

To convert from millilitres to microlitres, multiply the number of millilitres by 1,000:

$$0.05 \ mL \times 1,000 = 50 \ μL$$

4.27 b) Linear

A linear trend extends along a straight or nearly straight line.

4.28 d) 95%

For data distributed normally, 95% of data falls within two standard deviations of the mean.

4.29 a) 5.30–6.30

$$Upper \ limit = mean + (2 \times SD)$$

$$= 5.8 + (2 \times 0.25)$$

$$= 5.8 + 0.5$$

$$= 6.3$$

$$Lower \ limit = mean - (2 \times SD)$$

$$= 5.8 - (2 \times 0.25)$$

$$= 5.8 - 0.5$$

$$= 5.3$$

4.30 a) 62 mmol/L

First, multiply the standard deviation by 3 to get three standard deviations:

$$3 \times 3 = 9$$

Then add and subtract 9 from the mean to find the range:

$$72 + 9 = 81$$

$$72 - 9 = 63$$

Therefore, the range for 3 standard deviations is 63–81.

The only value that does not fall within this range is 62.

4.31 c) 3.9–5.5 mmol/L

A reference range of 95% includes all values two standard deviations below and above the mean.

First, find the value of two standard deviations. One standard deviation is 0.4, so two are 0.8 (0.4 × 2).

Next, find the range of values that fall within two standard deviations by adding and subtracting 0.8 from the mean:

$$\text{Upper limit} = \text{mean} + 2\text{SD}$$

$$= 4.7 + 0.8$$

$$= 5.5$$

$$\text{Lower limit} = \text{mean} - 2\text{SD}$$

$$= 4.7 - 0.8$$

$$= 3.9$$

Therefore, the range for two standard deviations is 3.9–5.5.

4.32 c) Standard deviation / mean

The coefficient of variation is calculated by dividing the standard deviation by the mean. For example, if the standard deviation is 3 and the mean is 30, the coefficient of variation is:

$$\frac{3}{30} = 0.1$$

The coefficient is often expressed as a percentage. The percentage is found by multiplying the result by 100:

$$0.1 \times 100 = 10\%$$

4.33 a) 15%

The equation for calculating the coefficient of variation is:

$$\text{coefficient of variation} = \frac{\text{SD}}{\text{mean}}$$

Inserting the values into the equation gives:

$$\text{coefficient of variation} = \frac{1.2}{8}$$

$$= 0.15$$

$$= 15\%$$

4.34 e) 6

The first step in calculating the mean is to add up the values:

$$2 + 2 + 5 + 7 + 14 = 30$$

Next, divide the total by the number of values:

$$\frac{30}{5} = 6$$

4.35 d) median

The median is the middle number in a sorted list of numbers. For example, if a data set contains the values 1, 2, 3, 4 and 4, then the mode is 3 because 3 is the middle number.

4.36 b) mean

The mean is calculated by adding all the values in a set and dividing the sum by the number of values.

4.37 c) 20

To work out the percent difference between two numbers, first, subtract the lower number from the higher number:

$$24 - 20 = 4$$

Then divide the difference (4) by the original number (20) to find the difference as a fraction:

$$\frac{4}{20} = 0.2$$

Finally, multiply the result by 100 to find the percentage:

$$0.2 \times 100 = 20\%$$

4.38 d) Reagent

Reagent grade (also known as analytical reagent grade) is for chemicals of the highest purity available for laboratory use. They typically have very low levels of impurities.

Commercial grade chemicals are the least pure and they often contain a significant amount of impurities.

Laboratory grade chemicals generally have a moderate level of purity.

Purified grade (also known as practical grade) typically implies a higher level of purity than commercial or technical grade, but they may not adhere to specific purity standards like analytical grade.

Technical grade chemicals have a lower level of purity compared to analytical grade. They may contain impurities that do not significantly affect their performance in industrial applications.

4.39 e) Results reported in the wrong units

Post-analytical errors occur after the specimen has been analyzed. Reporting the results in the wrong units is a post-analytical error because it occurs after analysis of the specimen.

4.40 b) ISO 15189

ISO 15189 is an international standard that specifies requirements for quality and competence in medical laboratories. This standard is designed to improve the quality of laboratory services and ensure the reliability of test results.

4.41 b) Number of improperly labelled samples

Pre-analytical quality indicators monitor the steps that happen before samples are analyzed in the laboratory. These steps include sample labelling, collection, transport, and preparation.

Improper labelling is an issue that occurs before analysis begins. Therefore the number of improperly labelled samples is a pre-analytical quality indicator.

4.42 e) Laboratory turnaround time

Turnaround time is a frequent quality assurance indicator in laboratories.

Turnaround time is the time it takes for the laboratory to analyze the specimens and dispatch the results.

4.43 e) repeatability or reproducibility of a procedure

Precision indicates how close results are to one another when a procedure is tested repeatedly. In other words, precision indicates the repeatability of a procedure.

The closeness of results to the true value is accuracy, not precision.

4.44 b) 97.0%

The formula to calculate diagnostic specificity is:

$$\frac{\text{true negatives}}{\text{true negatives} + \text{false positives}}$$

Inserting the values from the question into the formula:

$$= \frac{800}{800 + 25}$$

$$= \frac{800}{825}$$

$$= 0.970 (\text{to 3 s.f.})$$

$$= 97.0\%$$

4.45 e) specificity

Specificity is a test's ability to determine healthy cases correctly. The test shows high specificity because there were no false positives (no healthy patients were diagnosed as sick).

Sensitivity refers to a test's ability to determine sick cases correctly. The test shows low sensitivity because only 50% of sick people were correctly identified as sick.

Competency 5

Specimen Procurement, Processing and Data Collection

There are 67 questions in this competency.

5.1 When drawing blood from a frightened child, you should:
   a) bribe the child with candy
   b) explain the procedure to the child in simple terms
   c) say nothing to the child and just perform the procedure
   d) tell the child that the needle won't hurt
   e) tell the child to be brave

5.2 When drawing blood from an obese patient, which location should be the first place you look for a vein?
   a) The antecubital fossa
   b) The back of the hand
   c) The back of the knee
   d) The feet
   e) The neck

Answers on page 92

5.3 A patient has an arteriovenous (AV) fistula in his left arm and an IV in his right arm. From where should you draw a blood sample?

   a) Above the AV fistula

   b) Above the IV

   c) Below the AV fistula

   d) Below the IV

   e) From the IV

5.4 For venipuncture, tourniquets should be:

   a) applied very tightly to the arm

   b) left on the arm for at least three minutes

   c) removed after the needle is withdrawn

   d) tight enough to slow arterial flow

   e) tight enough to slow venous flow

5.5 What is the most common antiseptic used to disinfect the site before venipuncture?

   a) 70% isopropyl alcohol

   b) Betadine

   c) Bleach

   d) EMLA

   e) Iodine

5.6 When a blood pressure cuff is used for a venipuncture instead of a tourniquet, the pressure must be:

   a) between the patient's diastolic and systolic blood pressure

   b) equal to the patient's systolic blood pressure

   c) just above the patient's diastolic blood pressure

   d) just above the patient's systolic blood pressure

   e) just below the patient's diastolic blood pressure

Answers on page 92

5.7 What can happen if a phlebotomist releases the tourniquet after removing the needle from the arm?

a) Angina

b) Bleeding

c) Cyanosis

d) Edema

e) Paresthesia

5.8 What can happen if an angle of 35 degrees is used when performing venipuncture?

a) Nothing will happen as this is the correct angle

b) The needle may go completely through the vein

c) The needle may miss the vein completely

d) The needle will enter above the vein

e) The sample may be rejected due to hemolysis

5.9 What should you do if a patient faints during a venipuncture?

a) Continue the procedure until all blood is collected

b) Leave the needle in the vein and call the physician

c) Remove the needle and attend to the patient

d) Start artificial respiration immediately

e) Yell loudly at the patient to keep him conscious

5.10 In venipuncture, which of these actions may cause a hematoma?

a) Applying pressure to the puncture site after removing the needle

b) Asking the patient to form a fist so the veins are more prominent

c) Drawing blood from an arm that has an IV tube

d) Inserting the needle through the vein and puncturing the opposite wall

e) Removing the tourniquet before the needle is removed

Answers on page 93

5.11 Which of these is a sign of a needle puncturing an artery during venipuncture?

a) Blood spurting into the tube

b) Breathing difficulties

c) Dark blue blood

d) Dark yellow blood

e) Intense pain

5.12 A phlebotomist is performing a venipuncture. The needle is in place but no blood is entering the tube. What is the first thing the phlebotomist should do?

a) Change to pediatric tubes

b) Discontinue the draw and cancel the requisition

c) Push the needle in more deeply

d) Switch to a winged blood collection set

e) Try adjusting the needle slightly

5.13 A physician requests a vitamin A test and a complete blood count. In which vacutainer tubes should the phlebotomist collect the blood samples?

a) Gold and lavender

b) Gold and light blue

c) Grey and gold

d) Grey and lavender

e) Grey and light blue

5.14 What are cross-match tubes used for?

a) Blood alcohol testing

b) Blood compatibility testing

c) Coagulation studies

d) Glucose tests

e) Trace element studies

5.15 Green top vacutainers contain which anticoagulant?

a) Citrate

b) EDTA

c) Fluoride

d) Heparin

e) Oxalate

Answers on page 93

5.16 Which vacutainer tube is used for hemoglobin testing?

    a) Blue

    b) Green

    c) Grey

    d) Lavender

    e) Red

5.17 Which anticoagulant is in grey top vacutainers?

    a) EDTA

    b) Heparin

    c) Potassium oxalate

    d) SPS

    e) Sodium polyanethole sulfonate

5.18 The results of a comprehensive metabolic panel show decreased calcium levels and elevated potassium levels. All other results are normal. What is the most likely cause of the results?

    a) The patient is dehydrated

    b) The patient is taking excessive vitamin D supplements

    c) The sample was stored at room temperature

    d) The sample was taken from an arm with an intravenous drip

    e) The tube was contaminated with EDTA

5.19 What is the glycolytic inhibitor in grey top tubes?

    a) EDTA

    b) Heparin

    c) Silica

    d) Sodium citrate

    e) Sodium fluoride

5.20 Which vacutainer tube is used for trace metal analysis?

    a) Grey

    b) Light blue

    c) Orange

    d) Red

    e) Royal blue

Answers on page 94

5.21 Which colour vacutainer tube is known as the "SPS tube"?
   a) Gold
   b) Green
   c) Lavender
   d) Pink
   e) Yellow

5.22 Some royal blue top tubes contain _____ as an anticoagulant.
   a) EDTA
   b) lithium heparin
   c) potassium oxalate
   d) sodium citrate
   e) sodium heparin

5.23 Which vacutainer tube contains sodium citrate?
   a) Green
   b) Grey
   c) Light blue
   d) Pink
   e) Red (glass)

5.24 Which vacutainer tube contains no additives?
   a) Grey
   b) Pink
   c) Red (glass)
   d) Red (plastic)
   e) SST

5.25 Sodium fluoride preserves:
   a) cellulite
   b) cellulose
   c) glucose
   d) glycerin
   e) protein

Answers on page 94

5.26 What vacutainer tube is used for coagulation studies?

    a) Black

    b) Green

    c) Grey

    d) Light blue

    e) White

5.27 What vacutainer tube is used for reticulocyte counts?

    a) Green

    b) Grey

    c) Lavender

    d) Light blue

    e) Red

5.28 A phlebotomist needs to collect blood in a grey top tube, a gold top tube, and a lavender top tube. What is the correct order to fill the tubes?

    a) Gold, grey, lavender

    b) Gold, lavender, grey

    c) Grey, gold, lavender

    d) Grey, lavender, gold

    e) Lavender, gold, grey

5.29 Black top vacutainer tubes contain which anticoagulant?

    a) EDTA

    b) Lithium heparin

    c) Sodium citrate

    d) Sodium fluoride

    e) Sodium heparin

5.30 What additive prevents glycolysis in blood samples?

    a) EDTA

    b) Heparin

    c) Potassium oxalate

    d) Sodium citrate

    e) Sodium fluoride

Answers on page 95

5.31 A phlebotomist is performing venipuncture on a difficult vein using a butterfly. The phlebotomist has to collect an SST and a light blue top tube. How should the phlebotomist proceed?

   a) Collect the SST first then the light blue tube

   b) Collect the light blue tube first then the SST

   c) Draw a clear tube first, then collect the SST, then collect the light blue tube

   d) Draw a clear tube first, then collect the light blue tube, then collect the SST

   e) Draw half of the SST first, then collect the light blue tube, then finish the SST

5.32 What is the main purpose of tiger top tubes?

   a) Preventing clots

   b) Preventing glycolysis

   c) Separating plasma from blood cells

   d) Separating serum from blood cells

   e) Speeding up the formation of blood clots

5.33 Silica in vacutainer tubes:

   a) accelerates clotting

   b) destroys microorganisms

   c) inhibits thrombin

   d) preserves pH

   e) prevents glycolysis

5.34 Yellow top vacutainer tubes contain which anticoagulant?

   a) Acid citrate dextrose

   b) Potassium sorbate

   c) Sodium benzoate

   d) Sodium nitrite

   e) Sulphur dioxide

Answers on page 95

5.35 EDTA prevents blood clots by binding:
  a) calcium
  b) chloride
  c) plasma
  d) platelets
  e) red blood cells

5.36 What causes evacuated tubes to fill with blood automatically?
  a) Arterial blood pressure
  b) Gravity
  c) Pressure from the tourniquet
  d) Thermal insulation
  e) Vacuum in the tube

5.37 Which tool is needed to collect blood by syringe?
  a) Microhematocrit tube
  b) Multisample needle
  c) Transfer device
  d) Tube holder
  e) Winged infusion set

5.38 Which of these needles has the largest diameter?
  a) 18-gauge
  b) 19-gauge
  c) 20-gauge
  d) 21-gauge
  e) 22-gauge

5.39 The gauge size of a needle indicates the diameter of the needle's:
  a) bevel
  b) flange
  c) hub
  d) lumen
  e) shaft

Answers on page 95

5.40 Which part of a needle enters the skin first?

a) Bevel

b) Flange

c) Hub

d) Lumen

e) Shaft

5.41 Multisample needles are typically available in which gauges?

a) 18–20

b) 20–22

c) 22–24

d) 24–26

e) 26–28

5.42 When should you label a blood collection tube?

a) As soon as you receive the test order

b) Just before the patient arrives

c) Before you collect the specimen

d) After you collect the specimen

e) After the patient has left

5.43 If a patient is having blood drawn for a prothrombin time test, you might expect:

a) the patient to be fasting

b) the patient to bleed for a long time

c) the serum to be very lipemic

d) to have difficulty filling the tube

e) to have to mix the tube more

5.44 Why are gauze pads better than cotton balls for holding pressure on a puncture site?

a) Cotton balls can stick to the puncture site

b) Cotton balls contain latex which is dangerous for people with latex allergies

c) Cotton balls have a higher risk of causing a compression nerve injury

d) Gauze pads are more sterile

e) Gauze pads are significantly cheaper

Answers on page 96

5.45 Immediately after blood collection, how many times must tubes be inverted to ensure proper mixing of blood and additives?

  a) 1 or 2

  b) 8 to 10

  c) 10 to 15

  d) 15 to 20

  e) 20 to 30

5.46 Blood specimens for which test are placed in circles on special filter paper?

  a) Bilirubin

  b) Complete blood counts

  c) Malaria

  d) Phenylketonuria

  e) The isolation of fungi and mycobacteria

5.47 When whole blood is centrifuged in a grey top tube, what does it separate into?

  a) Plasma, buffy coat and red blood cells

  b) Plasma, clot, and red blood cells

  c) Red blood cells, white blood cells, and platelets

  d) Serum, buffy coat and red blood cells

  e) Serum, clot, and red blood cells

5.48 Which medication might cause a patient to bleed excessively from a venipuncture site?

  a) A herbal medicine

  b) An anticoagulant

  c) Birth control pills

  d) Insulin

  e) Medicine for high cholesterol

Answers on page 96

5.49 What is "the order of draw"?
- a) An order given by a superior to draw blood from a patient
- b) The correct sequence of steps for taking blood by venipuncture
- c) The order blood tubes are filled
- d) The order blood vials are stored
- e) The order you select patients to draw blood from

5.50 What is the best time to collect a sputum specimen?
- a) An hour before the patient has dinner
- b) In the late afternoon
- c) In the middle of the day
- d) Just after the patient wakes up
- e) Just before the patient goes to bed

5.51 Which of these tests is the most likely to require chain-of-custody documentation?
- a) Blood culture
- b) Cross-match
- c) Drug screen
- d) TDM
- e) Triglycerides test

5.52 PKU tests are performed routinely on:
- a) HIV patients
- b) cancer patients
- c) elderly patients
- d) new employees
- e) newborn infants

5.53 Which of these is an acceptable preservative for the phosphorus 24-hour urine test?
- a) Chlorhexidine
- b) Hydrochloric acid
- c) Sodium bicarbonate
- d) Sodium carbonate
- e) Sodium hydroxide

Answers on page 97

5.54 A patient is receiving a course of antibiotics. His last dose was at 2 pm. His next doses will be at 10 pm and 6 am. When is the best time to draw a blood culture?

   a) At 2 am
   b) At 6 am
   c) Immediately
   d) Just after his next dose
   e) Just before his next dose

5.55 How many bottles are drawn for a blood culture set?

   a) 1
   b) 2
   c) 3
   d) 4
   e) 5

5.56 Which of these actions is NOT performed when performing quality control of a glucometer?

   a) Apply a drop of blood to the test strip
   b) Check the test strips are in date
   c) Compare the result displayed by the glucometer with the expected value
   d) Insert a test strip into the glucometer
   e) Remove the test strip from the glucometer

5.57 Which fingers are used for finger puncture?

   a) Little finger and ring finger
   b) Little finger and thumb
   c) Middle finger and ring finger
   d) Ring finger and index finger
   e) Ring finger and thumb

Answers on page 97

5.58 Which part of an infant's foot is the safest area to perform a capillary puncture?

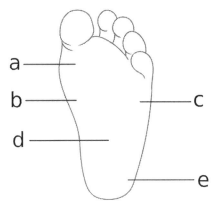

a) a
b) b
c) c
d) d
e) e

5.59 After a semen sample is collected, within how many hours must it be tested?
a) 1 hour
b) 6 hours
c) 12 hours
d) 24 hours
e) 72 hours

5.60 At what temperature are cryofibrinogen specimens transported?
a) −20°C or lower
b) 4–6°C
c) 21°C
d) 37°C
e) 55°C

Answers on page 98

5.61 Which of these specimens needs to be kept at 35–37°C?
   a) Blood culture
   b) Feces
   c) Sputum
   d) Throat swab
   e) Urine

5.62 Hemolysis of a blood specimen would NOT affect the result of which of these tests?
   a) Haptoglobin
   b) Iron
   c) MCHC
   d) Red blood cell count
   e) Total hemoglobin

5.63 Category B infectious substances must be shipped with a label that says:
   a) UN2814 – Infectious Substance, Category B, Affecting Humans
   b) UN3291 – Clinical Waste, Category B
   c) UN3373 – Biological Substance, Category B
   d) UN3549 – Communicable Disease, Category B, Affecting Humans
   e) UN3549 – Medical Waste, Category B, Affecting Humans

5.64 Which of these specimens is sterile in healthy people?
   a) Blood
   b) Feces
   c) Gastrointestinal tract specimens
   d) Sputum
   e) Urine

5.65 What colour is a positive result on the fecal occult blood test?
   a) Black
   b) Blue
   c) Green
   d) Red
   e) Yellow

Answers on page 98

5.66 Serum and plasma both contain:
  a) clotting factors
  b) plasma proteins
  c) platelets
  d) red blood cells
  e) white blood cells

5.67 The glycosylated hemoglobin test is used to diagnose which disease?
  a) Acidosis
  b) Diabetes
  c) Hemoglobin C disease
  d) Inflammation
  e) Renal disease

Answers on page 99

ANSWERS

5.1 b) explain the procedure to the child in simple terms

When drawing blood from a scared child, explain the procedure in simple terms. Be honest with the child; don't lie by telling them the needle won't hurt. It's also good to have the parent hold the child when you take the blood, as this can be comforting.

Saying nothing can be frightening for a child; it's important to communicate to reduce their anxiety.

Telling the child the needle won't hurt can erode the child's trust when they do experience pain.

Telling the child to be brave can add pressure and anxiety, making the child more nervous.

5.2 a) The antecubital fossa

When drawing blood from obese patients, check the antecubital area first. Obese patients often have an easily palpable median cubital vein.

5.3 d) Below the IV

Do not draw blood from an arm with an AV fistula. A blood draw could damage the fistula and cause infection or clotting.

Normally, arms with an IV should be avoided as well. However, since the left arm is out of the question and there is no better alternative, you should draw the blood from the patient's right arm. However, when drawing blood from an arm with an IV, make sure to draw below the IV. Never draw from a site above an IV or from the IV itself because the IV fluid will dilute the blood and affect the results.

5.4 e) tight enough to slow venous flow

The tourniquet should be tight enough to slow venous flow without affecting the arterial flow.

Option b (left on the arm for at least three minutes) is incorrect. Leaving the tourniquet on this long could cause blood pooling at the venipuncture site, leading to falsely elevated results.

Option c (removed after the needle is withdrawn) is incorrect because you should remove the tourniquet first then withdraw the needle.

5.5 a) 70% isopropyl alcohol

The most common antiseptic to cleanse and disinfect the site before venipuncture is 70% isopropyl alcohol in wipe form.

5.6 e) just below the patient's diastolic blood pressure

A blood pressure cuff for venipuncture should be inflated to a pressure just below the patient's diastolic blood pressure. This will restrict venous flow without stopping arterial flow.

5.7 b) Bleeding

If the needle is removed before the tourniquet, bleeding will occur around the puncture site.

5.8 b) The needle may go completely through the vein

An angle of 35 degrees is too steep and the needle may go completely through the vein. It's best to use an angle of 15 to 30 degrees instead.

5.9 c) Remove the needle and attend to the patient

If a patient faints during a venipuncture, the immediate priority is the patient's safety. Removing the needle prevents injury.

5.10 d) Inserting the needle through the vein and puncturing the opposite wall

A hematoma is a swollen or raised area at the venipuncture site resulting from the leakage of blood into the tissues. A hematoma can happen if the phlebotomist pushes the needle too far into and through the vein, causing blood to leak out of the vein and into the surrounding tissue.

Drawing blood from an arm in which there is an IV tube is not recommended because the fluid could dilute the results of the tests. However, it is unlikely to cause a hematoma.

5.11 a) Blood spurting into the tube

When an artery is punctured instead of a vein, blood will spurt into the tube due to the high pressure in arteries. Arterial blood is also brighter than venous blood because it has more oxygen.

Option e is incorrect because intense pain is more associated with accidental nerve puncture, not arterial puncture.

5.12 e) Try adjusting the needle slightly

If no blood flows when the needle is in place, then the needle may not be in a vein. You should first try slightly manipulating the needle. If blood still does not flow, you should withdraw the needle and repeat the procedure.

5.13 a) Gold and lavender

Vitamin A tests require gold tubes (also known as serum-separating tubes). These tubes contain a serum-separating gel that separates the serum from the rest of the blood. Gold tubes are used for many biochemistry tests, including vitamin tests.

Complete blood counts require lavender tubes. These tubes contain EDTA which prevents blood from clotting, which is important in complete blood counts.

5.14 b) Blood compatibility testing

Cross-match tubes are used for blood compatibility testing. The purpose of blood compatibility testing is to identify potential incompatibilities between the donor and recipient before blood transfusions.

5.15 d) Heparin

Green top vacutainers contain heparin as an anticoagulant. Heparin prevents blood clotting by inhibiting thrombin and other clotting factors.

5.16 d) Lavender

Lavender top tubes contain EDTA as an anticoagulant. These tubes are used for hemoglobin testing, complete blood counts, erythrocyte sedimentation rates, and blood typing.

5.17 c) Potassium oxalate

Grey top tubes contain potassium oxalate as an anticoagulant.

5.18 e) The tube was contaminated with EDTA

EDTA is an anticoagulant that works by binding to calcium. If EDTA comes into contact with a blood sample, it binds to the calcium ions, artificially lowering the calcium levels. EDTA also falsely increases potassium levels because EDTA contains potassium salts.

Because of this, blood for comprehensive metabolic panels must be collected in SST tubes or lithium heparin tubes, which do not contain EDTA.

5.19 e) Sodium fluoride

Sodium fluoride acts as a glycolytic inhibitor in grey top tubes by preventing the cells from using glucose.

EDTA is an anticoagulant, not a glycolytic inhibitor.

Silica is a coagulation activator, not a glycolytic inhibitor.

Sodium citrate and heparin are anticoagulants, not glycolytic inhibitors.

5.20 e) Royal blue

Royal blue top tubes are used for analysising trace metals, such as lead, arsenic, and cadmium.

5.21 e) Yellow

Yellow top tubes are called SPS tubes because they contain sodium polyanethol sulfonate. These tubes are used for blood bank studies, human leukocyte antigen phenotyping, DNA testing, and paternity testing.

5.22 a) EDTA

Royal blue top tubes can contain EDTA, which prevents blood from clotting by binding to calcium ions.

5.23 c) Light blue

Light blue top tubes contain sodium citrate as an anticoagulant. Sodium citrate prevents blood from clotting by binding to calcium.

5.24 c) Red (glass)

Red-top glass tubes contain no clot activators, anticoagulants, preservatives, or separator material.

Grey top tubes potassium oxalate as an anticoagulant and sodium fluoride as a preservative.

Pink top tubes contain EDTA as an anticoagulant.

Red plastic tubes contain a clot activator.

SST (gold top) tubes contain a clot activator and serum gel separator.

5.25 c) glucose

Sodium fluoride preserves glucose in blood samples. It inhibits glycolysis (the process by which cells break down glucose), ensuring the measured glucose levels are accurate.

5.26 d) Light blue

Coagulation tests use light blue top vacutainer tubes. These tubes contain sodium citrate which acts as an anticoagulant by binding to calcium ions in the blood. Sodium citrate is used because it is easily reversible: when the laboratory is ready to perform the test, calcium is added back to the sample, which starts the coagulation cascade.

5.27 c) Lavender

Lavender tubes are used for hematology tests, such as complete blood counts, platelet counts, sedimentation rate, and reticulocyte counts.

5.28 b) Gold, lavender, grey

Gold tubes are filled before lavender tubes, and grey tubes are always filled last.

5.29 c) Sodium citrate

Black top tubes are used for sedimentation rate tests. They contain sodium citrate as the anticoagulant.

5.30 e) Sodium fluoride

The additive sodium fluoride is used to prevent glycolysis in blood samples. Sodium fluoride acts as a glycolysis inhibitor by inhibiting the enzyme enolase in the glycolytic pathway. This helps maintain the glucose levels in the blood sample, ensuring that glucose measurements are accurate when tested. This is important for glucose tests.

5.31 d) Draw a clear tube first, then collect the light blue tube, then collect the SST

If a winged blood collection device (butterfly) is used to collect a light blue top tube, a waste (clear) tube should be drawn first to remove the air in the tubing of the butterfly. If the air is not removed first, then the air will be drawn into the light blue tube, which will affect the blood-to-anticoagulant ratio and cause erroneous results.

Furthermore, the light blue tube must be drawn before the SST, to avoid the clot activator in the SST from contaminating the light blue tube.

5.32 d) Separating serum from blood cells

Tiger top tubes are coloured red and grey, like the stripes of a tiger. They separate serum from blood cells for tests requiring serum. They are the equivalent of gold top tubes.

5.33 a) accelerates clotting

Silica is a clot activator. Some vacutainer tubes have silica sprayed on the inner walls of the tube to accelerate the clotting process.

5.34 a) Acid citrate dextrose

Yellow-topped tubes are used for special tests using whole blood. They contain acid citrate dextrose as an anticoagulant. These tubes are also known as SPS tubes because they also contain the additive sodium polyanethol sulfonate.

5.35 a) calcium

EDTA binds with the calcium ions in the blood, preventing the blood from clotting.

5.36 e) Vacuum in the tube

Evacuated tubes used in blood collection fill with blood automatically due to the vacuum in the tube. When the needle is inserted into a vein, the vacuum in the tube pulls blood into it without the need for additional pressure or external forces.

5.37 c) Transfer device

Syringes are used to collect blood from patients with small or fragile veins. Blood collected in syringes is then transferred into the vacutainer tubes using a blood transfer device.

Microhematocrit tubes are used for collecting blood for hematocrit tests.

Multisample needles are for collecting blood several samples with a single puncture.

5.38 a) 18-gauge

The smaller the needle gauge, the larger the diameter.

5.39 d) lumen

The lumen is the hollow bore that runs the length of the needle.

5.40 a) Bevel

The bevel of the needle is the sharp tip. It is the part of the needle that enters the skin first.

5.41 b) 20–22

Multisample needles are used for drawing multiple blood samples. They are typically available in 20 to 22 gauge sizes. These sizes are optimal for allowing adequate blood flow while minimizing discomfort.

5.42 d) After you collect the specimen

The best time to label a specimen is immediately after collection, in the presence of the patient. This helps to ensure accurate patient specimen identification.

You should never label a blood collection tube before collecting the specimen because this could result in a mislabeled specimen.

5.43 b) the patient to bleed for a long time

The prothrombin time (PT) test evaluates blood clotting. A doctor would order a PT test if the patient bleeds excessively.

5.44 a) Cotton balls can stick to the puncture site

Pressure should be applied using a clean gauze pad instead of cotton balls. This is because fibres from cotton balls can stick to the puncture site and dislodge the platelet plug when removed.

5.45 b) 8 to 10

The general advice is to invert the tube 8 to 10 times.

5.46 d) Phenylketonuria

Phenylketonuria (PKU) is the abnormal build-up in the body of a protein called phenylalanine. The blood specimens for phenylketonuria are placed on filter paper before analysis.

5.47 a) Plasma, buffy coat and red blood cells

Grey top tubes contain an anticoagulant to prevent blood from clotting. When blood with an anticoagulant is spun in a centrifuge, it separates into three layers:

1. Plasma (the liquid when an anticoagulant prevents clotting)
2. Buffy coat (white blood cells and platelets)
3. Red blood cells

Serum forms if blood is allowed to clot.

5.48 b) An anticoagulant

Anticoagulants reduce the ability of the blood to clot, which can cause excessive bleeding.

5.49 c) The order blood tubes are filled

The "order of draw" is the recommended sequence in which blood collection tubes should be filled during phlebotomy to prevent cross-contamination of additives between tubes.

5.50 d) Just after the patient wakes up

The best time for a patient to collect a sputum specimen is first thing in the morning, which is when mucus and phlegm are at their highest levels.

5.51 c) Drug screen

Chain of custody is recommended whenever there is a risk a sample could be tampered with and and the test results have legal consequences. An example is a drug screen. Drug screens are sometimes used by companies to test employees for illegal drug use. Drug screens are also used by sporting bodies to test athletes for performance-enhancing drugs. In these cases, the testing specimen may require chain-of-custody documentation to prove the sample was not tampered with.

5.52 e) newborn infants

Phenylketonuria (PKU) is a rare but potentially serious disorder. Babies are usually tested for PKU at around five days old. The test involves pricking the baby's heel to collect drops of blood.

5.53 b) Hydrochloric acid

Phosphorus 24-hour urine tests may not require a preservative. However, if a preservative is used, then it must be an acid such as hydrochloric acid (HCl) or sulfamic acid.

5.54 e) Just before his next dose

If blood cultures must be drawn during a course of antibiotics, it is recommended to draw the blood culture just before the next dose of antibiotics is due. This ensures that the antibiotic levels in the blood are at their lowest, allowing for the highest possible yield of bacteria in the blood culture. and providing a better chance of detecting any bacterial growth.

In this case, considering the patient's next dose is at 10 pm, the optimal time to draw the blood culture would be right before the 10 pm dose.

5.55 b) 2

Two bottles are drawn for a blood culture set: an aerobic bottle and an anaerobic bottle.

Typically, a phlebotomist will draw two sets (meaning four bottles) from two different venipuncture sites. This improves the chances of detecting an infection while also helping to identify potential contamination.

5.56 a) Apply a drop of blood to the test strip

Glucometer quality control does not use blood. A control solution is used instead.

5.57 c) Middle finger and ring finger

Finger punctures should be done on the middle finger or ring finger.

The little finger is not recommended for finger punctures because it has less tissue, increasing the risk of hitting bone during puncture.

The thumb and index finger are more sensitive than other fingers and may have calluses or scars, making them unsuitable for finger punctures.

5.58 e) e

The best place to take blood from an infant's foot is the most lateral portion of the plantar surface of the heel, which is option e. This is generally a safe place to perform an infant capillary puncture because the fat here is thickest.

5.59 a) 1 hour

Sperm motility and other parameters rapidly decline once semen is out of the body. For this reason, semen samples are typically analyzed within one hour of collection.

5.60 d) 37°C

Cryofibrinogen specimens are transported at body temperature (37°C). Cryofibrinogen clumps together at temperatures below normal body temperature, leading to inaccurate test results.

5.61 a) Blood culture

Blood cultures detect the presence of microorganisms in the blood. Blood culture specimens should never be refrigerated or frozen. Cold temperatures can inhibit or kill the microorganisms in the blood sample.

In contrast, most other specimens (urine, sputum, swabs, etc.) can be stored in the refrigerator for several hours before culturing.

5.62 e) Total hemoglobin

Hemolysis (the destruction of red blood cells) affects the results of most blood tests. For tests like iron, potassium, magnesium, and phosphorous, hemolysis increases the result, because when red blood cells break down, they release their constituents into the surrounding serum or plasma.

Hemolysis would not affect total hemoglobin however, because total hemoglobin is a measure of the total amount of hemoglobin inside red blood cells plus the amount of hemoglobin outside red blood cells. Therefore, any hemoglobin released from the hemolyzed red blood cells still contributes to the total hemoglobin measurement.

Hemolysis falsely decreases haptoglobin levels because haptoglobin will bind to the free hemoglobin released from the lysed red blood cells.

Hemolysis falsely increases the MCHC (mean corpuscular hemoglobin concentration).

Hemolysis falsely decreases red blood cell counts because of the destruction of red blood cells.

5.63 c) UN3373 – Biological Substance, Category B

The proper shipping name of a Category B infectious substance is *UN3373, Biological Substance, Category B*. This shipping name must appear on the outer container.

5.64 a) Blood

Of the options, only blood is normally sterile. The detection of microbes in the blood is therefore always abnormal.

5.65 b) Blue

The fecal occult blood test detects blood in the stool. A small sample of stool is placed on a chemically treated card. If the card turns blue, the stool is positive for occult blood. If the card does not change colour, the stool is negative for occult blood.

5.66 b) plasma proteins

Plasma is the liquid part of blood and contains plasma proteins, clotting factors, electrolytes, antibodies, antigens, and hormones. Serum is the same as plasma except serum does not contain clotting factors. Therefore "plasma proteins" is the correct answer as plasma proteins are found in both plasma and serum.

Answer a is incorrect as clotting factors are only found in plasma, not serum.

Answers c and d are incorrect as platelets and red blood cells are found in neither plasma nor serum.

Answer e is incorrect as white blood cells are also found in neither plasma nor serum.

5.67 b) Diabetes

A glycosylated hemoglobin test (also called A1c or HbA1c) measures the amount of glucose in the blood. It can be used to diagnose diabetes.

Competency 6

Laboratory Safety

There are 52 questions in this competency.

6.1 "Insidious" hazards are hazards that:
    a) are easily overlooked
    b) are unpreventable
    c) happen quickly
    d) involve chemicals
    e) involve fumes

6.2 What is the word for an inanimate object that can transmit infectious agents from one individual to another?
    a) Adenovirus
    b) Bacteria
    c) Fomite
    d) Germ
    e) Parasite

6.3 A toxic chemical that affects the body by being absorbed into the blood is called a blood:
    a) agent
    b) antagonist
    c) antibody
    d) attacker
    e) panel

Answers on page 112

6.4 How should you pick up an item of hot glassware?
  a) By pouring cold water on it to cool it down
  b) Using latex gloves
  c) With a rag or paper towels
  d) With tongs
  e) With your hands

6.5 Which of these actions helps prevent the release of aerosols in the laboratory?
  a) Filling centrifuge tubes to the brim
  b) Forcibly expelling hazardous materials from pipettes
  c) Opening aerosol containment devices immediately after removing them from the centrifuge
  d) Routinely inspecting the centrifuge to ensure there is no leakage
  e) Using tubes with cracks in them

6.6 Used needles should be discarded in:
  a) a biohazard autoclave bag
  b) a biohazard sharps container
  c) a glass disposal bucket
  d) a glass recycling bin
  e) the regular garbage

6.7 Which of these is an example of passive fire protection?
  a) Auto-closing ventilation in fume cupboards
  b) Fire alarms
  c) Fire extinguishers
  d) Fire-resistant walls
  e) Sprinklers

Answers on page 112

6.8 What is an upper flammability limit?
   a) The amount of fuel that will burn before the fuel burns itself out
   b) The highest concentration of a chemical that can catch fire
   c) The highest temperature at which a chemical can be stored safely
   d) The highest temperature at which a chemical fire will ignite
   e) The lowest temperature at which a chemical will ignite

6.9 Refer to the image below:

Another name for this type of fire extinguisher is a
_____ fire extinguisher.
   a) ABC
   b) AFFF foam
   c) carbon dioxide
   d) class F
   e) wet powder

Answers on page 113

6.10 At low concentrations, what does hydrogen sulfide smell like?

    a) Burnt sugar

    b) Cherries

    c) Rotten eggs

    d) Rotting meat

    e) Strong cheese

6.11 What is the term for chemicals that cause birth defects in embryos and fetuses?

    a) Carcinogens

    b) Corrosives

    c) Immunogens

    d) Phenyls

    e) Teratogens

6.12 A lab assistant accidentally drinks a beaker of Zenker's fluid. He says he feels a burning sensation in his mouth and throat. The lab manager phones 911. While waiting for the ambulance to arrive, which of these other first-aid measures should be taken?

    a) Ask the lab assistant to remove his contact lenses

    b) Give the lab assistant water to drink

    c) Place the lab assistant in the recovery position

    d) Take the lab assistant outside for fresh air

    e) Tell the lab assistant to rinse his eyes with water for several minutes

6.13 Mixing bleach with acid produces water, salt and:

    a) arsenic trioxide

    b) chlorine gas

    c) hydrogen cyanide

    d) phosgene

    e) sodium cyanide

Answers on page 113

6.14 What is the correct order of removal of PPE?
    a) Gloves, gown, goggles, mask
    b) Gown, goggles, gloves, mask
    c) Gown, mask, gloves, goggles
    d) Mask, gloves, goggles, gown
    e) Mask, gown, gloves, goggles

6.15 In which of these situations should safety goggles be worn?
    a) During blood collections
    b) During reagent and specimen preparation
    c) When talking to members of the public
    d) While inspecting reagent supplies
    e) While transporting sealed waste containers

6.16 Which of these helps protect against non-ionizing radiation?
    a) Biosafety cabinet
    b) Fire extinguisher
    c) Fume hood
    d) Goggles
    e) Laboratory-safe refrigerator

6.17 The three basic protective measures against radiation are time, distance, and:
    a) exposure
    b) lead
    c) radiation suit
    d) shielding
    e) speed

6.18 You find a colleague unconscious and not breathing. There is no one around to help. What is the first thing you should do?
    a) Call 911
    b) Find a defibrillator
    c) Give chest compressions
    d) Give mouth-to-mouth breaths
    e) Move your colleague into the recovery position

Answers on page 114

6.19 What should you do if someone is having a seizure?

    a) Give chest compressions

    b) Give mouth-to-mouth breaths

    c) Hold them down

    d) Put something soft under their head

    e) Put something wooden in their mouth

6.20 People at risk of a severe allergic reaction often carry devices that inject which medication?

    a) Acetaminophen

    b) Adrenaline

    c) Fluticasone

    d) Insulin

    e) Morphine

6.21 When should you NEVER administer care to a casualty?

    a) When the person has stopped breathing

    b) When the person is an organ donor

    c) When the person is having a seizure

    d) When the person is unconscious

    e) When the person refuses care

6.22 The recovery position is used for patients who are:

    a) breathing abnormally

    b) conscious and breathing normally

    c) unconscious and not breathing

    d) unconscious but breathing normally

    e) undergoing cardiac arrest

6.23 If you suspect someone has suffered a stroke, what is the first thing you should do?

    a) Apply pressure to the affected area

    b) Ask the person to lie down

    c) Contact emergency services

    d) Loosen items of tight clothing

    e) Perform CPR

Answers on page 114

6.24 You find a person lying on the floor. You suspect they
have received an electric shock. What is the first thing you
must do before treating them?

   a) Check if the person is breathing
   b) Check if the person is still in contact with the electrical
      current
   c) Check the person's pulse
   d) Make a note in the incident logbook
   e) Wrap the person in a thermal blanket

6.25 In CPR, how many chest compressions should be given per
second?

   a) 1
   b) 2
   c) 3
   d) 4
   e) 5

6.26 Which of the following is the correct sequence of events in
the chain of survival?

   a) Call 911, defibrillation, start CPR
   b) Call 911, start CPR, defibrillation
   c) Defibrillation, call 911, start CPR
   d) Defibrillation, start CPR, call 911
   e) Start CPR, call 911, defibrillation

6.27 A lab technologist has spilled concentrated hydrochloric
acid onto his clothing and skin, affecting a large portion of
his body. After he has removed his clothing, the next thing
he should do is:

   a) apply a burn ointment to his skin
   b) apply bandages
   c) pour baking soda onto his skin
   d) seek emergency medical assistance
   e) use the emergency safety shower

Answers on page 115

6.28 A colleague has cut his lower arm and is bleeding. Which of the following is NOT an appropriate response?

a) Apply firm pressure to the wound using sterile gauze

b) Clean and dress the wound once the bleeding has stopped

c) Place a tourniquet over the elbow joint

d) Tell your colleague to keep his arm raised

e) Wear gloves

6.29 The Heimlich maneuver is used for:

a) choking

b) heart attack

c) heat stroke

d) poisoning

e) syncope

6.30 What is the first action to take if someone goes into cardiac arrest?

a) Assess the airway

b) Call 911

c) Check the pulse

d) Perform chest compressions

e) Put the person into the supine position

6.31 What is the single most important method of preventing infection?

a) Proper handwashing

b) Sneezing into your arm

c) Thorough cleaning of equipment

d) Wearing a lab coat

e) Wearing protective goggles

6.32 Universal precautions apply to which type of hazard?

a) Bloodborne pathogens

b) Dangerous chemicals

c) Environmental hazards

d) Fire

e) Radiation

Answers on page 115

6.33 What is post-exposure prophylaxis?
  a) A delayed allergic reaction to an allergen
  b) An auto-immune disease
  c) The inability to breathe after exposure to an allergen
  d) The protocol for cleaning a laboratory after the release of a dangerous pathogen
  e) Treatment after exposure to a pathogen to prevent infection from occurring

6.34 Which of these is an OPIM (other potentially infectious material)?
  a) Feces
  b) Saliva
  c) Semen
  d) Urine
  e) Vomit

6.35 The six links in the chain of infection are infectious agent, reservoir, portal of exit, mode of transmission, portal of entry, and:
  a) behaviour
  b) hospital-acquired infection
  c) reagent
  d) susceptible host
  e) vaccination

6.36 Bottles of organic peroxides require which two pictograms?
  a) Corrosion and exclamation mark
  b) Flame and exploding bomb
  c) Flame and flame over a circle
  d) Health hazard and exclamation mark
  e) Health hazard and gas cylinder

6.37 Gases under pressure have a pictogram of:
  a) a flame
  b) a flame over a circle
  c) a gas cylinder
  d) an exploding bomb
  e) an exploding test tube

Answers on page 116

6.38 If the word 'Forbidden' is written in column 3 of a Hazardous Materials Table, it means the material should not be:

a) discarded

b) ingested

c) picked up

d) transported

e) used

6.39 Which cleaning product releases a toxic gas when mixed with urine?

a) Chlorine bleach

b) Hydrogen peroxide

c) Isopropyl alcohol

d) Povidone-iodine

e) Sodium hydroxide

6.40 Ethanol can NOT kill:

a) E. coli

b) Pseudomonas aeruginosa

c) Salmonella typhosa

d) fungi

e) spores

6.41 Which colour on the NFPA hazard diamond signals the degree of hazards to health?

a) Blue

b) Green

c) Red

d) White

e) Yellow

6.42 What is the NFPA colour code for flammable hazards?

a) Blue

b) Green

c) Red

d) White

e) Yellow

Answers on page 116

6.43 The cabinet with the highest personal, environmental, and specimen protection is the:

    a) class A biological safety cabinet

    b) class I biological safety cabinet

    c) class II biological safety cabinet

    d) class III biological safety cabinet

    e) fume hood

6.44 What virus causes hepatitis C?

    a) HAV

    b) HBC

    c) HCC

    d) HCV

    e) HPC

6.45 Class 7 materials in the Transportation of Dangerous Goods Act are:

    a) corrosive

    b) explosive

    c) flammable or combustible

    d) poisonous or infectious

    e) radioactive

6.46 Specimens containing the smallpox virus must be transported as:

    a) Category A

    b) Category B

    c) Class 1

    d) Class 2

    e) exempt

6.47 Which class of dangerous goods are flammable solids?

    a) 1

    b) 2

    c) 3

    d) 4

    e) 5

Answers on page 117

6.48 What are the three GHS hazard classes?
a) Biological, chemical, and radiation
b) Electrical, fire, and chemical
c) Health, physical, and environmental
d) Physical, psychosocial, and psychological
e) Slips, trips, and falls

6.49 According to the GHS Hazard Classification, which of these is a type of physical hazard?
a) Carcinogenicity
b) Eye effects
c) Flammable gases
d) Skin corrosion
e) Skin irritation

6.50 According to the American National Standards Institute (ANSI), which sign indicates a potential hazard that could result in minor or moderate injury?
a) Caution
b) Danger
c) Notice
d) Risk
e) Warning

6.51 What worldwide system gives recommendations on how to label hazardous chemicals?
a) GHS
b) HCS
c) HPR
d) HazCom
e) WHMIS

6.52 Who or what does protective isolation protect?
a) A patient
b) Lab equipment
c) Laboratory samples
d) Medical personnel
e) The general public

Answers on page 117

ANSWERS

6.1 a) are easily overlooked

Insidious hazards are dangers that are not obvious and are therefore easily overlooked. They are usually not easily seen, tasted, smelled, or felt. Examples of insidious hazards are aerosols, carcinogens, fumes, and radiation.

6.2 c) Fomite

Fomites are inanimate objects that can carry and spread disease and infectious agents. Examples of fomites in the laboratory are countertops, handrails, doorknobs, light switches, and phones.

6.3 a) agent

A blood agent is a toxic chemical agent that affects the body by being absorbed into the blood.

6.4 d) With tongs

Hot glassware should always be handled with tongs to avoid burns. Using a rag or paper towels can be ineffective and dangerous.

Latex gloves do not provide sufficient heat protection.

6.5 d) Routinely inspecting the centrifuge to ensure there is no leakage

Leaking or broken tubes can release aerosols during centrifugation. If the centrifuge itself is damaged or cracked, these aerosols can then escape into the laboratory air. Therefore, you should regularly inspect centrifuges for cracks, fissures, and holes.

Option b is incorrect because pipettes should be left to drain. Forcibly expelling hazardous material from a pipette can create dangerous aerosols.

Option c is incorrect because aerosol containment devices should be opened in a biological safety cabinet after removal from the centrifuge. If a biological safety cabinet is unavailable, you should wait at least 10 minutes before opening the aerosol containment device.

6.6 b) a biohazard sharps container

Used venipuncture needles are considered biohazardous sharps. Therefore they must be discarded into a designated sharps container. This helps prevent needle-stick injuries.

6.7 d) Fire-resistant walls

Passive fire protection is built into the structure of the building and includes structural features such as fire-resistant walls, doors and floors.

Active fire protection requires something to turn it on. Examples are alarms, sprinkler systems, and auto-closing ventilation in fume cupboards. Active fire protection is inherently less reliable than passive protection in that it requires a trigger to turn it on.

6.8 b) The highest concentration of a chemical that can catch fire

The upper flammability limit of a substance is the highest concentration that can burn. At higher concentrations, the substance will not burn due to insufficient oxygen.

In contrast, the lower flammability limit of a substance is the lowest concentration that can burn.

6.9 a) ABC

The image shows a dry powder fire extinguisher. These fire extinguishers are also known as ABC fire extinguishers because they can extinguish class A, B, and C fires.

Dry powder fire extinguishers smother the fire with phosphate-based powder like a blanket, depriving the fire of oxygen. These extinguishers can extinguish wood and paper fires (class A), liquid fires (class B), and electrical fires (class C).

6.10 c) Rotten eggs

Hydrogen sulfide is a colorless, flammable gas that smells like rotten eggs at low concentrations. It has a sickening sweet smell at high concentrations.

6.11 e) Teratogens

Teratogens are chemicals that cause birth defects in developing embryos and fetuses.

6.12 b) Give the lab assistant water to drink

If someone swallows a poisonous liquid, you should immediately give them water or milk to drink. Water can help reduce the burning sensation in the mouth and throat while diluting the poison. The exception is if they have symptoms that make it hard to swallow (such as vomiting, convulsions, or a decreased level of alertness).

Taking the lab assistant outside for fresh air is appropriate for exposure by inhalation, not ingestion.

6.13 b) chlorine gas

Chlorine gas is a dangerous byproduct of mixing bleach with acid. The gas is deadly in high concentrations. For this reason, bleach and acid should never be mixed.

6.14 a) Gloves, gown, goggles, mask

The general strategy is to remove PPE from the most contaminated to the least contaminated. You should remove gloves first as these are most likely to be contaminated since they have come in contact with lab equipment. The gown should be removed next as this may have received splashes during the lab work. Goggles and masks can be removed last are they are the least likely to be contaminated.

6.15 b) During reagent and specimen preparation

Safety goggles must be worn when handling reagents and specimens. Goggles help to protect the eyes from chemicals, biological materials, and other dangerous substances.

Option a is incorrect because safety goggles are not typically required for blood collections, as there is little to no risk of blood splashing,

Option d is incorrect because safety goggles are generally unnecessary when inspecting inventory.

Option e is incorrect because safety goggles are not needed to carry sealed waste containers.

6.16 d) Goggles

Commonly used PPE against non-ionizing radiation are UV safety goggles, UV face shields, and gloves. Skin protection is not difficult, as most clothing tends to absorb UV radiation.

6.17 d) shielding

Time, distance, and shielding measures minimize exposure to radiation.

6.18 a) Call 911

The first thing you should do is call 911. By calling 911 first, you ensure trained professionals are on the way. Also, the 911 dispatcher can guide you through the process of performing CPR while you wait for the ambulance to arrive.

6.19 d) Put something soft under their head

Putting something soft under the head of a person having a seizure can protect the head from bumps.

Chest compressions are for cardiac arrest.

Mouth-to-mouth breaths are for someone who is not breathing.

You should never try to hold down someone having a seizure as this can cause an injury.

You shouldn't put anything into the mouth of someone having a seizure as this can injure their teeth or the jaw.

6.20 b) Adrenaline

Adrenaline is the first treatment for severe allergic reactions (anaphylaxis). It is available in a pre-loaded injection device known as an adrenaline auto-injector. Adrenaline acts quickly to open up the airways, reduce their swelling and raise blood pressure.

6.21 e) When the person refuses care

Never administer care to a casualty who explicitly refuses care. Casualties have the right to refuse first aid treatment and their wishes need to be respected

6.22 d) unconscious but breathing normally

The recovery position is for people who are unconscious but still breathing. The position keeps their airway open and prevents choking.

The other options (breathing abnormally, cardiac arrest, and unconscious and not breathing) require CPR instead.

6.23 c) Contact emergency services

When someone has suffered a stroke, it is crucial to call 911 as quickly as possible. Prompt treatment can significantly improve outcomes for stroke patients.

6.24 b) Check if the person is still in contact with the electrical current

If you suspect someone has received an electric shock, you must ensure they are no longer in contact with the electrical current before you can treat them. If possible to do so safely, you should turn off the source of electricity. DO NOT touch the casualty if you have been unable to isolate them from the source of the electrical shock or turn off the electricity, or you will receive a shock yourself.

6.25 b) 2

Chest compressions should be delivered at a rate of 100 to 120 per minute, or around two compressions per second.

6.26 b) Call 911, start CPR, defibrillation

The "chain of survival" is the sequence of events that maximizes the chances of survival from cardiac arrest. The correct sequence is:

1. Call 911 to get emergency services on their way

2. Start CPR to maintain circulation and oxygenation

3. Use defibrillation to restore a normal heart rhythm

6.27 e) use the emergency safety shower

In the case of an acid spill to the body, the immediate priority should be to rinse the affected area with water to remove as much water as possible. If a large part of the body is affected, the emergency safety shower should be used.

6.28 c) Place a tourniquet over the elbow joint

When someone is bleeding, applying a tourniquet should be a last resort. This is because tourniquets can permanently damage nerves, muscles, and blood vessels, and even result in the loss of the extremity. Therefore tourniquets should only be used as a last resort when all other methods of controlling the bleeding have failed.

Furthermore, tourniquets should never be applied on a joint. Placing a tourniquet over a joint can reduce its effectiveness in stopping bleeding. It can also cause nerve, bone, and tissue damage.

Telling your colleague to keep his arm raised is a good idea because this will reduce blood flow to his arm and help stop the bleeding.

6.29 a) choking

The Heimlich maneuver is an emergency procedure for upper airway obstructions (choking). By exerting pressure on the bottom of the diaphragm, the lungs are forced to expel air, dislodging the obstruction.

6.30 b) Call 911

The sooner the person is seen by paramedics and gets to the emergency room, the better the chance of survival. This is why it is important to call 911 as quickly as possible.

6.31 a) Proper handwashing

Handwashing is generally considered the most important procedure for preventing infection. Hands come into contact with surfaces and objects throughout the day, picking up pathogens. Washing your hands with soap and water removes the pathogens, preventing their spread.

6.32 a) Bloodborne pathogens

Universal precautions are a standard set of guidelines to prevent the transmission of bloodborne pathogens.

6.33 e) Treatment after exposure to a pathogen to prevent infection from occurring

Post-exposure prophylaxis (PEP) is medication taken after potential exposure to a pathogen. The medication prevents the pathogen from establishing itself in the body and causing infection. The most common type of PEP is against HIV.

6.34 c) Semen

Other potentially infectious material (OPIM) is dangerous because it may contain bloodborne pathogens. OPIMs include semen, vaginal secretions, blood, and several internal body fluids.

Sweat, tears, saliva, urine, feces, and vomit are not considered OPIMs unless they contain visible blood.

6.35 d) susceptible host

The chain of infection describes the process of how an infection spreads. The steps are

1. infectious agent (virus, parasite, fungus, or bacterium)
2. reservoir (the environment where a pathogen can live and multiply)
3. portal of exit (how the pathogen leaves the reservoir)
4. mode of transmission (how a pathogen moves from the reservoir to a host)
5. portal of entry (where the pathogen enters the host, such as mouth, eyes, and wounds)
6. susceptible host (the person at risk of infection)

Breaking any link in this chain helps prevent the spread of infection.

6.36 b) Flame and exploding bomb

When heated, organic peroxides may cause fire or explosion. Therefore, they require the flame and exploding bomb pictograms.

6.37 c) a gas cylinder

The gas cylinder pictogram (shown in Figure 1) is a gas cylinder in a red diamond. This pictogram is for gases under pressure. Gases under pressure are dangerous because they can release large amounts of gas into the air quickly.

Figure 1: The gas cylinder pictogram.

6.38 d) transported

Column 3 is the class of the material to be transported. The word "Forbidden" in this column means that the dangerous good must not be transported.

6.39 a) Chlorine bleach

Chlorine reacts with the ammonia in urine to form chloramine. Chloramine is a toxic gas that can cause coughing, irritation, and, in severe cases, death. For this reason, chlorine-based disinfectants should never be used on urine spills.

6.40 e) spores

Spores are difficult to kill. Methods that normally kill bacteria, such as ethanol, are ineffective at killing them.

6.41 a) Blue

On the NFPA hazard diamond, the health hazard is blue, the flammability hazard is red, and the reactivity hazard is yellow.

6.42 c) Red

The red section of the NFPA diamond symbol represents the fire hazard rating of a material. NFPA stands for the National Fire Protection Association.

6.43 d) class III biological safety cabinet

Biosafety cabinets are divided into three classes: I, II and III. The class that provides the best protection is class I.

6.44 d) HCV

HCV stands for hepatitis C virus.

6.45 e) radioactive

Class 7 materials in the Transportation of Dangerous Goods Act refer to radioactive substances. These materials require special handling during transport.

6.46 a) Category A

The smallpox virus is a Category A infectious substance. This means it can cause permanent disability or life-threatening disease to humans or animals. Therefore it must always be shipped as Category A.

Category B is for less serious infectious substances that do not generally cause permanent disability or life-threatening disease.

Classes 1–9 are for hazardous materials in general, such as explosives and flammable liquids.

6.47 d) 4

Class 4 dangerous goods are flammable solids. These materials easily ignite during transport.

6.48 c) Health, physical, and environmental

The Globally Harmonized System of Classification and Labelling of Chemicals (GHS) uses three hazard classes: health hazards, physical hazards, and environmental hazards.

6.49 c) Flammable gases

Flammable gas is classified as a physical hazard due to its potential to ignite and cause fires. The other options are classified as health hazards.

6.50 a) Caution

Caution signs are for hazards that could cause minor or moderate injury.

Warning signs and danger signs are for more dangerous hazards. These are hazards that could cause serious injury or death.

6.51 a) GHS

GHS stands for Globally Harmonized System. It is the worldwide set of best practices for classifying and labelling chemicals.

The other answers are incorrect because they are not worldwide:

Hazard Communication Standard (HCS) is only used in the United States.

Hazardous Products Regulations (HPR) is only used in Canada.

HazCom is only used in the United States.

WHMIS is only used in Canada.

6.52 a) A patient

Protective isolation (or reverse isolation) protects immunocompromised patients from contracting infections from other people.

A different type of isolation known as enteric isolation protects the public from patients with dangerous contagious diseases.

Competency 7

Laboratory Equipment

There are 30 questions in this competency.

7.1 A lab assistant has just finished washing an item of
glassware with water when the supervisor comes over and
says she needs the glassware right away. To dry the
glassware quickly, the lab assistant should rinse it with:
  a) acetic acid
  b) acetone
  c) hydrochloric acid
  d) hydrogen peroxide
  e) sodium nitrate

7.2 What is the best way to clean glassware containing
water-insoluble solutions?
  a) Rinse 2-3 times with ethanol then rinse 3-4 times with
      deionized water
  b) Rinse 3-4 times with deionized water
  c) Rinse with copious amounts of tap water then rinse 3-4
      times with deionized water
  d) Wash with hot soapy water
  e) Wash with hot soapy water, rinse thoroughly with tap
      water, and then rinse 3-4 times with deionized water

Answers on page 125

7.3 Which of the following plastics is autoclavable?

a) High density polyethylene

b) Low density polyethylene

c) Polypropylene

d) Polystyrene

e) Polyurethane

7.4 Which item of lab equipment sterilizes using pressurized steam?

a) Alcohol

b) Autoclave

c) Dry heat sterilizer

d) Fume hood

e) Oven

7.5 Autoclave tape changes colour when:

a) organisms have been killed

b) sterilization has taken place

c) the autoclave is nearing the end of its warranty

d) the autoclave reaches a specific temperature

e) there are spores remaining

7.6 Autoclaving uses what method of sterilization?

a) Chemical

b) Dry heat

c) Moist heat

d) Physical

e) Radiation

7.7 Which type of glass is autoclavable?

a) Annealed

b) Borosilicate

c) Float

d) Lead

e) Soda-lime

Answers on page 125

7.8 Which of these can NOT be autoclaved?

    a) Gloves

    b) Microbial growth media

    c) Organic solvents

    d) Stainless steel

    e) Tissue culture flasks

7.9 A lab assistant is wrapping an instrument for autoclaving but discovers the wrapper has a hole. What should the lab assistant do?

    a) Get a new wrapper

    b) Ignore the hole and continue wrapping the instrument

    c) Repair the hole with adhesive tape

    d) Throw both the instrument and the wrapper away

    e) Throw the instrument away

7.10 Which of these biomarkers can urine refractometers measure?

    a) The presence of nitrates in urine

    b) Urine colour

    c) Urine hemoglobin concentration

    d) Urine osmolality

    e) Urine specific gravity

7.11 Which item of lab equipment uses high-speed rotation in a closed chamber?

    a) Autoclave

    b) Centrifuge

    c) Evaporator

    d) Hot plate

    e) Shaker

7.12 Which of these is a container used for heating substances over a Bunsen burner?

    a) Beaker

    b) Crucible

    c) Erlenmeyer flask

    d) Funnel

    e) Graduated cylinder

Answers on page 126

7.13 Which of the following solutions is used to calibrate pH meters?

a) Buffer solution

b) Deionized water

c) Distilled water

d) Sodium chloride solution

e) Sodium hydroxide solution

7.14 Type 1 glass is:

a) aluminosilicate

b) borosilicate

c) fused silica

d) lead

e) soda-lime

7.15 Automated blood cell counters work on which principle?

a) Boyle

b) Campbell

c) Coulter

d) Ferguson

e) McKenzie

7.16 Which water purification destroys microorganisms but does not filter out unwanted minerals and ions?

a) Double distillation

b) Ion exchange column

c) Reverse osmosis

d) Ultrafiltration

e) Ultraviolet radiation

7.17 Which part of a microscope adjusts the light intensity?

a) Iris diaphragm

b) Numerical aperture

c) Objective lens

d) Ocular lens

e) Stage clip

Answers on page 126

7.18 The _____ is a measure of a microscope's
ability to gather light and resolve fine specimen detail.
- a) contrast
- b) empty magnification
- c) lens power
- d) numerical aperture
- e) objective

7.19 What part of a microscope focuses light onto the specimen?
- a) Aperture
- b) Condenser
- c) Diaphragm
- d) Objective lens
- e) Ocular lens

7.20 Microscopes usually have which objective lenses?
- a) 10x, 40x, and 100x
- b) 10x, 50x, and 100x
- c) 20x, 40x, and 80x
- d) 20x, 50x, and 80x
- e) 20x, 50x, and 100x

7.21 Which pipette is the most accurate?
- a) Bulb
- b) Graduated
- c) Pasteur
- d) Vacuum-assisted
- e) Volumetric

7.22 Which of these glass types has the strongest resistance to
heat?
- a) Borosilicate
- b) Crystal
- c) Lead
- d) Optical
- e) Soda-lime

Answers on page 127

7.23 Volumetric glassware has the letters TC inscribed on it because it:

a) can hold toxic chemicals

b) contains a fixed volume

c) delivers a fixed volume

d) is Type C glassware

e) is good at controlling temperatures

7.24 What does "10 mL TD 25 SEC" on a pipette mean?

a) The pipette can be filled with 10 mL in 25 seconds

b) The pipette can deliver 10 mL in its primary tube and 25 mL in its secondary tube

c) The pipette holds 10 mL and has a diameter of 25 mm

d) The pipette will deliver 10 mL when left to drain for 25 seconds

e) You should wait 25 seconds between filling and dispensing the pipette

7.25 Which kind of centrifuge is used to spin capillary tubes?

a) Angle head

b) Cytospin

c) Gas

d) Microhematocrit

e) Refrigerated

7.26 Which kind of centrifuge has good cellular morphology preservation?

a) Angle head

b) Cytocentrifuge

c) Microhematocrit

d) Refrigerated

e) Ultracentrifuge

7.27 Cytocentrifuges are also known as:

a) basic centrifuges

b) cell centrifuges

c) cytospins

d) low-angle centrifuges

e) ultracentrifuges

Answers on page 127

7.28 Which type of centrifuge is optimized for spinning a rotor at very high speeds and is capable of generating acceleration as high as 1,000,000 g?

a) Clinical centrifuge

b) Cytocentrifuge

c) High-speed centrifuge

d) Microcentrifuge

e) Ultracentrifuge

7.29 What is the most common cause of excessive centrifuge vibration?

a) Electrical interference

b) Excessive temperature

c) Unbalanced tubes

d) Uneven bench surfaces

e) Variable voltage

7.30 The two electrodes of a pH meter are called the
_____ electrodes.

a) capacitive and potentiated

b) dry and wet

c) glass and reference

d) negative and positive

e) sealed and ground

Answers on page 128

ANSWERS

7.1 b) acetone

Adding acetone to wet glassware lowers the surface tension of the water and helps the water to evaporate quickly.

7.2 a) Rinse 2-3 times with ethanol then rinse 3-4 times with deionized water

Water alone cannot remove water-insoluble solutions from glassware. For this reason, the glassware first needs to be rinsed with a solvent such as acetone or ethanol.

7.3 c) Polypropylene

Out of the choices, only polypropylene is safe to autoclave. The other plastics could melt in the autoclave and ruin the autoclave chamber.

7.4 b) Autoclave

Autoclaves sterilize equipment by subjecting it to pressurized steam. In comparison, dry heat sterilizers and ovens use hot air for sterilization.

7.5 d) the autoclave reaches a specific temperature

Autoclave tape shows that a specific temperature has been reached.

Sterilization indicators, not autoclave tape, show if sterilization has taken place. Sterilization indicators are placed inside the pack and indicate the sterility of the contents.

7.6 c) Moist heat

Autoclaving uses moist heat under pressure to sterilize. It is one of the most effective sterilization methods because it kills all microbial life forms, including spores.

7.7 b) Borosilicate

Borosilicate glass has a high resistance to temperature change, making it suitable for autoclaving. For this reason, borosilicate glass is commonly used in laboratory equipment, such as beakers, flasks, and test tubes, which are often sterilized in autoclaves.

Annealed glass is the weakest type of glass because it has not been heat-strengthened or fully tempered. It would break in an autoclave.

Lead glass is not considered to be autoclavable. This is because lead glass is highly susceptible to thermal shock and can easily break or crack under the high temperatures and pressure used in autoclave sterilization.

Soda-lime glass, also known as float glass, is not highly resistant to thermal shock and is therefore not recommended for use in autoclaves.

7.8 c) Organic solvents

Organic solvents, such as alcohol, acetone, benzene, and toluene, cannot be autoclaved. They are volatile and/or flammable. Therefore they could catch fire in the autoclave.

Other things that cannot be autoclaved are acids, bases, chlorides, sulphates, chlorine, hypochlorite, bleach, non-stainless steel, and some plastics, including polystyrene, polyethylene, and polyurethane.

7.9 a) Get a new wrapper

If a lab assistant discovers that the wrapper for an instrument has a hole before autoclaving, the instrument should not be sterilized in that wrapper. This is because the hole may allow microorganisms to enter the package during sterilization, leading to contamination of the instrument. Instead, the lab assistant should use a new wrapper to package the instrument for autoclaving.

7.10 e) Urine specific gravity

Urine refractometers can measure the specific gravity, refraction index, and serum content (the amount of serum) of urine.

7.11 b) Centrifuge

Centrifuges rotate quickly to separate liquids into their components.

7.12 b) Crucible

A laboratory crucible is a container that can endure extremely high temperatures. It is used for heating substances over a Bunsen burner.

7.13 a) Buffer solution

A buffer solution is a solution that resists changes in pH when small amounts of acid or base are added to it. Buffer solutions are used for calibrating pH meters because they have a known, stable pH and pH meters need to be calibrated using known pH values.

Water can not be used to calibrate ph meters because it does not contain enough ions for the pH electrode to give an accurate reading.

7.14 b) borosilicate

Type 1 glass is a type of borosilicate glass. It is a type of glass commonly used in laboratories due to its high resistance to thermal shock and its ability to withstand rapid temperature changes.

7.15 c) Coulter

Automated blood cell counters work on the Coulter Principle, a principle based on detecting changes in electrical resistance as a particle or cell goes through a small aperture.

7.16 e) Ultraviolet radiation

Ultraviolet light is highly effective at eliminating bacteria, viruses, and other microorganisms from water. However, UV light does not remove any other contaminants from water such as heavy metals, salts, and minerals.

7.17 a) Iris diaphragm

The diaphragm (also called the iris diaphragm) adjusts the size and intensity of the light that reaches the specimen. It is located within the condenser and consists of thin metal or plastic blades that can be adjusted to vary the size of the aperture. By adjusting the iris diaphragm, the amount of light that passes through the specimen can be controlled, which can help to optimize the contrast and resolution of the image.

7.18 d) numerical aperture

The numerical aperture of a lens is its ability to collect and focus light. It is usually between 0 and 1. Higher values mean better light-gathering, resolving power, and detail clarity.

7.19 b) Condenser

The condenser is a lens that focuses light on the specimen. It is used with higher magnifications.

7.20 a) 10x, 40x, and 100x

Most microscopes have a low-power objective lens (10×), a high-power objective lens (40×), and an oil immersion objective lens (100×).

7.21 e) Volumetric

The most accurate type of pipette is a volumetric pipette. Volumetric pipettes have a single graduation mark and are designed to dispense a single, precise volume of liquid, typically to an accuracy of ±0.02%.

7.22 a) Borosilicate

Borosilicate glass is very resistant to heat. It will not crack under extreme temperature changes. This makes it the glass of choice in laboratories for beakers, vials, test tubes, and flasks.

Lead glass has a low melting temperature. It is used mainly for electrical applications because of its electrical-insulating properties.

Soda-lime glass becomes soft when heated. For this reason, it is also known as soft glass.

7.23 b) contains a fixed volume

TC is an abbreviation for "to contain". It means that the capacity printed on the pipette is the same as the amount of liquid it can hold.

7.24 d) The pipette will deliver 10 mL when left to drain for 25 seconds

10 mL indicates the volume the pipette is designed to deliver.

TD stands for "to deliver,", meaning the specified volume is delivered after draining.

25 SEC is the time the pipette should be drained to ensure accurate delivery of the full 10 mL.

7.25 d) Microhematocrit

Capillary tubes are small, thin tubes used for collecting or separating small amounts of blood. They are spun in microcentrifuges, a type of centrifuge ideal for spinning small volumes of samples, such as microcentrifuge tubes, PCR tubes, and capillary tubes.

7.26 b) Cytocentrifuge

A cytocentrifuge is a special centrifuge that concentrates cells in fluid specimens onto a microscope slide so that they can be stained and examined. It has better preservation of cell morphology than other centrifuges.

7.27 c) cytospins

Cytocentrifuges, also called cytospins, are specialized centrifuges designed to separate cells in body fluids so they can be examined.

7.28 e) Ultracentrifuge

An ultracentrifuge is a centrifuge optimized for spinning a rotor at very high speeds, capable of generating acceleration as high as 1,000,000 g. They are commonly used in molecular biology, biochemistry, and cell biology, to separate small particles such as viruses, viral particles, proteins and protein complexes.

7.29 c) Unbalanced tubes

The most common cause of excessive centrifuge vibration is unbalanced sample tubes. Even a slight weight imbalance between samples will cause the centrifuge to vibrate and shake. The centrifuge can even explode in extreme circumstances.

7.30 c) glass and reference

The two electrodes of a pH meter are the glass and reference electrodes.

Competency 8

Histology and Cytology

There are 21 questions in this competency.

8.1 What is the term for formaldehyde dissolved in water?
   a) Acetone
   b) Cytospray
   c) Eosin
   d) Ethyl acetate
   e) Formalin

8.2 In histology, which of these chemicals is used for fixation?
   a) Chloroform
   b) Formalin
   c) Increasing strengths of alcohol
   d) Paraplast
   e) Xylene

8.3 Which of these actions will prevent the formation of acid formaldehyde hematin in formaldehyde solutions?
   a) Adding drops of cytochrome b5 reductase
   b) Keeping the solutions refrigerated
   c) Placing the solutions in 70% alcohol overnight
   d) Using buffered formalin
   e) Washing excess fixative overnight with water

Answers on page 134

8.4 What is the correct order of steps to process tissue containing calcium?

a) Decalcification, dehydration, fixation, clearing, infiltration

b) Decalcification, dehydration, fixation, infiltration, clearing

c) Dehydration, fixation, infiltration, decalcification, clearing

d) Fixation, decalcification, dehydration, clearing, infiltration

e) Fixation, dehydration, decalcification, infiltration, clearing

8.5 What happens if tissue is left in xylene for more than three hours?

a) The tissue becomes a milky colour

b) The tissue becomes brittle

c) The tissue becomes red

d) The tissue swells in size

e) The xylene becomes solid

8.6 Paraffin wax should be used at _____ its melting point.

a) 5–10°C below

b) 2–3°C below

c) the same temperature as

d) 2–3°C above

e) 5–10°C above

8.7 An advantage of paraffin wax embedding is:

a) it preserves fats

b) rapid diagnosis

c) samples can be stored long-term

d) sections can be cut ultra-thin

e) tissue can be viewed without a microscope

Answers on page 134

8.8 What is the melting point of Paraplast?

 a) 52–56°C

 b) 62–66°C

 c) 72–76°C

 d) 82–86°C

 e) 92–96°C

8.9 Which microtome is used to prepare tissue sections for electron microscopy?

 a) Cryostat

 b) Hand microtome

 c) Rotary microtome

 d) Sledge microtome

 e) Ultramicrotome

8.10 Which freezing technique is the coldest?

 a) Aerosol sprays

 b) Carbon dioxide gas

 c) Carbon dioxide 'cardice'

 d) Isopentane cooled by liquid nitrogen

 e) Liquefied nitrogen

8.11 A lab technician has cut a ribbon of sections from a tissue block. What should the lab technician do next?

 a) Add a few drops of a softening agent

 b) Float the sections on warm water

 c) Leave the sections at room temperature for 30 minutes

 d) Leave the sections in a freezer for an hour

 e) Submerge the sections in ethanol

8.12 Diamond blades are needed to cut:

 a) bone

 b) brain tissue

 c) intestinal tissue

 d) muscle tissue

 e) skin tissue

Answers on page 135

8.13 Wax sections are typically cut how thick during microtomy?

    a) 4–10 nm

    b) 40–100 nm

    c) 4–10 µm

    d) 4–10 mm

    e) 40–100 mm

8.14 For electron microscopy, sections must be about _____ times thinner than sections for light microscopy.

    a) 2

    b) 20

    c) 200

    d) 2,000

    e) 20,000

8.15 Before staining, paraffin sections must be:

    a) dewaxed

    b) left underwater for at least an hour

    c) refrigerated

    d) submerged in a chlorine solution

    e) warmed in an oven

8.16 In the hematoxylin and eosin (H&E) staining method, the eosin stains:

    a) connective tissue blue

    b) cytoplasms pink

    c) microorganisms blue

    d) nuclei blue

    e) nuclei pink

8.17 The most common mordant for H&E staining is:

    a) Alcian blue

    b) alum

    c) eosin

    d) hematoxylin

    e) sodium metabisulphite

Answers on page 135

8.18 What cell structure turns blue in H&E staining?

    a) Cytoplasm

    b) Golgi apparatus

    c) Mitochondria

    d) Nuclei

    e) Reticulum

8.19 _____ staining is the process of staining living cells that have been removed from the body.

    a) Differential

    b) Gram

    c) In vivo

    d) Positive

    e) Supravital

8.20 When a smear is too red, neutrophil granules look:

    a) blue-red

    b) brilliant red

    c) green

    d) indistinct

    e) light blue

8.21 Which cytological technique involves passing a urine sample through a biological filter containing pores of a specific diameter?

    a) Centrifugation

    b) Clean-catch

    c) Flow cytometry

    d) Millipore filtration

    e) Urine culture

Answers on page 135

ANSWERS

8.1 e) Formalin

Formaldehyde dissolved in water is commonly referred to as formalin. Formalin is a commonly used fixative for preserving biological tissues.

8.2 b) Formalin

Formalin is the universal fixative in routine histology.

Chloroform is used for clearing.

Increasing strengths of alcohol are used for dehydration.

Paraplast is used for embedding.

Xylene is used for clearing and deparaffinizing.

8.3 d) Using buffered formalin

With formaldehyde solutions, the formaldehyde can break down to form formic acid, which reacts with hemoglobin to produce an artifact pigment (acid formaldehyde hematin). However, this can be prevented by using buffered formalin.

8.4 d) Fixation, decalcification, dehydration, clearing, infiltration

The steps for tissue processing are typically fixation, dehydration, clearing, and wax infiltration. However, tissues containing calcium also need to be decalcified to remove the calcium. Decalcification comes after fixation and before dehydration.

Therefore the correct sequence is:

- Fixation: fix the tissue to preserve it
- Decalcification: decalcify the tissue to remove calcium deposits
- Dehydration: remove that water from the tissue
- Clearing: Replace the dehydration agent with a clearing agent
- Infiltration: Replace the clearing agent with paraffin wax

8.5 b) The tissue becomes brittle

Xylene is a common solvent used in histology to remove the water from tissue samples, making them more transparent and allowing for easier processing and embedding in paraffin wax. However, if tissue is left in xylene for too long, the tissue can become over-dehydrated and brittle.

8.6 d) 2–3°C above

Paraffin wax should be used at a temperature 2–3°C above its melting point for infiltration and embedding. This temperature melts the paraffin wax so it can be used to infiltrate and embed tissue samples.

If the temperature is too high, it can cause the paraffin wax to evaporate or become too thin, which can lead to poor tissue infiltration and embedding. If the temperature is too low, the paraffin wax may solidify and become difficult to work with, leading to poor sectioning and staining of tissue samples.

8.7 c) samples can be stored long-term

One of the main benefits of paraffin wax embedding is that it allows for long-term storage of tissue samples.

8.8 a) 52–56°C

Paraplast is a wax used for tissue infiltration. It melts between 52 and

56°C.

8.9 e) Ultramicrotome

Ultramicrotomes cut sections extremely thin (about 200 times thinner than wax sections) for use in electron microscopy.

8.10 e) Liquefied nitrogen

Liquid nitrogen is the coldest freezing technique, with a temperature of around –195.8°C.

8.11 b) Float the sections on warm water

After sectioning, the cut tissue is floated over a water bath to eliminate wrinkles and distortion in the tissue.

8.12 a) bone

Diamond knives are used to slice hard materials such as bone, teeth, and tough plant matter.

8.13 c) 4–10 μm

Microtomy is the technique of cutting tissues into sections. Wax blocks are typically cut into sections from 4 to 10 micrometers (μm) in thickness. This thickness is optimal for light microscopy, allowing for detailed examination of cellular structures.

8.14 c) 200

Electron microscopy sections are about 200 times thinner than those for light microscopy. The sections must be extremely thin to allow the electrons to pass through the sample and create an image.

8.15 a) dewaxed

Dewaxing is necessary to remove paraffin before staining.

8.16 b) cytoplasms pink

Eosin is a pink stain. It binds to cytoplasmic proteins, collagen, and some extracellular matrix proteins, turning them pink.

Hematoxylin is a blue dye that binds to DNA and RNA, turning nuclei blue or purple.

8.17 b) alum

The most common mordant used for H&E staining is aluminum ammonium sulphate (alum). The mordant helps the dye to stick to the nuclei.

8.18 d) Nuclei

The hematoxylin in H&E has a deep blue-purple colour that stains nucleic acids blue.

8.19 e) Supravital

Supravital staining (also called in vitro staining) is the process of staining living cells that have been removed from the body.

In vivo staining (also called intravital staining) is the process of staining living cells that are still inside the body.

8.20 b) brilliant red

If a smear is too red, neutrophil granules will appear bright red.

8.21 d) Millipore filtration

A millipore filter has a controlled pore size. It filters out large particles from a solution while letting smaller particles pass through. This makes it useful in urine cytology.

A clean catch is a method of collecting urine samples.

Flow cytometry is a technology that uses lasers to analyze cells or particles as they flow past.

A urine culture is a technique for revealing the causative microorganism for UTIs.

Competency 9

Clinical Microbiology

There are 40 questions in this competency.

9.1 What is the counterstain in Gram's technique?
   a) Acetone-alcohol
   b) Crystal violet
   c) Giemsa
   d) Iodine
   e) Safranin

9.2 In acid-fast staining, what colour are acid-fast bacteria?
   a) Blue
   b) Green
   c) Red
   d) White
   e) Yellow

9.3 When exposed to acid, acid-fast bacteria:
   a) decolourize at the same rate as other bacteria
   b) decolourize faster than other bacteria
   c) decolourize more slowly than other bacteria
   d) do not decolourize
   e) move faster

Answers on page 146

9.4 Which of these is needed for a malaria test?

a) Agar

b) Capillary tube

c) Clay sealant

d) Glass slide

e) Microhematocrit tube

9.5 A sample for the respiratory syncytial virus (RSV) test is best collected using a:

a) cough plate

b) expectorated sputum

c) nasal aspirate

d) throat swab

e) tracheal tube

9.6 What colour does the indicator strip inside a GasPak chamber turn when oxygen is present?

a) Black

b) Blue

c) Colourless

d) Red

e) Yellow

9.7 Smears of cerebrospinal fluid (CSF) are prepared with:

a) centrifuged CSF sediment

b) filtered CSF sediment

c) filtered CSF supernatant

d) incubated CSF supernatant

e) uncentrifuged CSF supernatant

9.8 Which test detects antibodies to the Epstein-Barr virus?

a) C-reactive protein test

b) Erythrocyte sedimentation rate

c) Influenza test

d) Monospot test

e) Rapid Group A Streptococcus test

Answers on page 146

9.9 Skin scrapings are set up in microbiology to identify:

a) Corynebacterium

b) Escherichia coli

c) Neisseria

d) fungi

e) small cell lung cancer

9.10 What is the usual temperature for an incubator used for culture and sensitivity?

a) 15–17°C

b) 25–27°C

c) 35–37°C

d) 45–47°C

e) 55–57°C

9.11 Which fluorescent dye glows green under blue light?

a) Alexa Fluor

b) Chromomycin A3

c) DAPI

d) GFP

e) Rhodamine

9.12 Which of the following incubation conditions is used to grow Streptococcus pneumoniae?

a) At 35–37°C, over 3 days in chocolate agar or MacConkey agar, with 20% H_2

b) At 35–37°C, overnight in media containing blood and sugar, with 5–10% CO_2

c) At 42°C, over 2 days in media containing electrolytes and peptone water, and under microaerophilic conditions

d) At 42°C, over 3 days in Luria Bertani agar, and under anaerobic conditions

e) At 42°C, over 3 days in mannitol salt agar, with 15–20% O_2

Answers on page 146

9.13 Bacteria that are NOT acid-fast are termed:
  a) acid-slow
  b) acidophilic
  c) alkaline-fast
  d) alkaliphilic
  e) non-acid-fast

9.14 What is the goal of streaking an agar plate?
  a) To accelerate the solidification of the agar medium
  b) To determine if the bacteria can ferment glucose, sucrose and/or lactose
  c) To determine the number of organisms in the sample
  d) To produce isolated colonies for further study
  e) To produce dense growth which covers the plate

9.15 Which ingredient in Thayer-Martin agar suppresses the growth of fungi?
  a) Nystatin
  b) Polymyxin
  c) Colistin
  d) Vancomycin
  e) Agar

9.16 What is reducing media used for in microbiology?
  a) Cultivating organisms that only grow in blood
  b) Growing anaerobic bacteria
  c) Isolating fungi and yeasts
  d) Reducing the pH of broth or agar
  e) Testing pathogens for antibiotic susceptibility

9.17 Which enzyme is used to make digest of blood?
  a) Amylase
  b) Lactase
  c) Lipase
  d) Pepsin
  e) Trypsin

Answers on page 147

9.18 CLED agar lacks electrolytes to prevent the swarming of which species?

a) Proteus

b) Pseudomonas

c) Shigella

d) Vibrio

e) Yersinia

9.19 What does modified Thayer-Martin agar contain that Thayer-Martin agar does not?

a) Nystatin

b) Peptone water

c) Potassium dihydrogen phosphate

d) Trimethoprim lactate

e) Vancomycin

9.20 In an agar slant tube, what is the poorly oxygenated area at the bottom of the tube called?

a) Bed

b) Butt

c) Foot

d) Pith

e) Root

9.21 Which of these are found in all agar media?

a) Distilled water and electrolytes

b) Gelatin and sugar

c) Seaweed and dissolved oxygen

d) Vitamins and blood

e) pH indicators and gelling properties

9.22 What type of broth is used to differentiate between aerobes and anaerobes?

a) Glucose

b) Lysogeny

c) Selenite F

d) Thioglycolate

e) Tryptic soy

Answers on page 147

9.23 Which of these types of agar is used to isolate and differentiate species of Salmonella and Shigella?

a) Hektoen enteric

b) Chocolate

c) CLED

d) Thayer Martin

e) MacConkey

9.24 Blood for blood agar plates is usually obtained from which animal?

a) Dogs

b) Goats

c) Pigs

d) Rabbits

e) Sheep

9.25 What is the sequence of steps for Gram staining?

a) Primary stain, counterstain, mordant, decolourizing

b) Primary stain, decolourizing, counterstain, mordant

c) Primary stain, decolourizing, mordant, counterstain

d) Primary stain, mordant, counterstain, decolourizing

e) Primary stain, mordant, decolourizing, counterstain

9.26 In Gram staining, what can happen if the decolourizer is left on too long?

a) All organisms will appear colourless

b) Gram-negative organisms will get lysed

c) Gram-negative organisms will look gram-positive

d) Gram-positive organisms will look gram-negative

e) No cells will appear on the slide

9.27 What can happen if the heat fixation step is skipped in Gram staining?

a) All organisms will appear colourless

b) All organisms will appear gram-negative

c) All organisms will appear gram-positive

d) Gram-negative organisms will appear Gram-positive, and vice versa

e) No cells will appear on the slide

Answers on page 148

9.28 What is the final step in acid-fast staining?
a) Add a drop of sterile water to a clean slide
b) Cover the smear with the counterstain
c) Cover the smear with the primary stain
d) Decolourize the smear with alcohol
e) Heat fix the smear

9.29 Which acid-fast staining method is known as the hot method?
a) Auramine-Rhodamine
b) Fluorochrome
c) Kinyoun
d) Truant
e) Ziehl-Neelsen

9.30 What characteristic helps identify mycobacteria?
a) Acid-fastness
b) Alpha hemolytic
c) Anaerobic
d) Gram negative
e) Motile

9.31 What is the term for bacterial cells used to start a new culture on a streak plate?
a) Colonies
b) Inoculum
c) Isolated colonies
d) Prime culture
e) T cells

9.32 Agar plates are placed upside down in the incubator to prevent:
a) contamination from other agar plates
b) gas bubbles from escaping
c) moisture from accumulating on the agar surface
d) pathogens from overgrowing
e) the medium from drying out

Answers on page 148

9.33 When performing a quadrant streak plate, what action must be taken after streaking each quadrant?
a) Allow the colonies to rest for 15–20 seconds
b) Flame the inoculating loop
c) Incubate the plate
d) Invert the plate
e) Take another loopful of inoculum from the original sample

9.34 When a quadrant streak plate is streaked correctly, which quadrant has the most cells?
a) All quadrants should have the same number of cells
b) Quadrant 1
c) Quadrant 2
d) Quadrant 3
e) Quadrant 4

9.35 A lab assistant is culturing a strain of Streptococcus pyogenes which produces streptolysin O. After streaking the blood plate, what special measure should the lab assistant perform to detect this hemolysin?
a) Add methylene blue
b) Connect the plate to a Durham tube
c) Invert the plate 8–10 times
d) Pour nutrient broth over the agar
e) Stab the agar

9.36 What is the term for bacteria that need high levels of carbon dioxide?
a) Capnophile
b) Carbonophile
c) Carbophile
d) Caseophile
e) Coprophile

Answers on page 149

9.37 Obligate anaerobes are killed by:

   a) carbon dioxide

   b) light

   c) nitrogen

   d) oxygen

   e) water

9.38 Which of these is a microaerophilic environment?

   a) 10% O_2

   b) 21% O_2

   c) 35% O_2

   d) 42% O_2

   e) 55% O_2

9.39 What is the term for an organism that does not need oxygen?

   a) Aerobe

   b) Anaerobe

   c) Antiaerobe

   d) Microaerophile

   e) Obligate aerobe

9.40 Which media is used to transport and preserve stool specimens?

   a) Anaerobic media

   b) Blood agar

   c) Cary-Blair media

   d) Lowenstein-Jensen agar

   e) MacConkey agar

Answers on page 149

ANSWERS

9.1 e) Safranin

Safranin is the counterstain in Gram's technique. It is applied after decolourization to give a pink-red colour to the gram-negative bacteria.

Acetone-alcohol is a decolourizing agent used to remove the crystal violet dye from the gram-negative bacteria.

Crystal violet is the primary stain used in Gram's technique.

Gram's iodine fixes the primary stain.

9.2 c) Red

Acid-fast bacteria appear red while non-acid-fast bacteria appear blue/green.

9.3 d) do not decolourize

Acid-fast bacteria are resistant to decolourization. Under a microscope, they appear red because they still have the carbolfuchsin stain.

9.4 d) Glass slide

The malaria test requires a drop of blood on a glass slide. The slide is then stained and examined under a microscope.

9.5 c) nasal aspirate

The respiratory syncytial virus (RSV) causes respiratory tract infections. A nasal wash or aspirate is the most common way to collect a sample for RSV testing because it gives the most accurate results.

9.6 b) Blue

Indicator strips turn deep blue in the presence of atmospheric oxygen and colourless when oxygen is gone.

9.7 a) centrifuged CSF sediment

Cerebrospinal fluid (CSF) smears are prepared by placing 12 drops of centrifuged CSF sediment onto a slide.

9.8 d) Monospot test

The mononucleosis spot test (also known as the Monospot test or heterophile antibody test) is a blood test that determines whether a patient has antibodies to the Epstein-Barr virus, which is a virus that causes infectious mononucleosis.

9.9 d) fungi

Skin, hair, and nail tissue are collected in microbiology to establish whether the patient has a fungal infection.

9.10 c) 35–37°C

Human pathogens grow best at body temperature (37°C). This is why incubators for C&S are kept at 37°C.

9.11 d) GFP

GFP stands for green fluorescent protein. It exhibits bright green fluorescence when exposed to blue light.

9.12 b) At 35–37°C, overnight in media containing blood and sugar, with 5–10% CO_2

Streptococcus pneumoniae grows best at 37°C (body temperature) in media containing blood and sugar. 5–10% CO in its environment promotes growth and hemolysis. It should be cultivated for no longer than 24 hours.

9.13 e) non-acid-fast

Acid-fast bacteria have a waxy cell wall that retains certain stains even when treated with acid. Bacteria that do not have this property are termed non-acid-fast.

9.14 d) To produce isolated colonies for further study

Streaking an agar plate is used to isolate individual microbial colonies, making it easier to study and identify the microorganism.

9.15 a) Nystatin

The ingredient in Thayer-Martin agar that inhibits the growth of fungi is nystatin.

Colistin and polymyxin inhibit the growth of gram-negative bacteria except for Neisseria.

Vancomycin inhibits the growth of gram-positive bacteria.

Agar is the solidifying agent. It does not suppress the growth of organisms.

9.16 b) Growing anaerobic bacteria

Reducing media are used for growing anaerobic bacteria in the laboratory. The media contains agents that remove oxygen from the culture medium and thereby create an anaerobic environment.

9.17 d) Pepsin

The enzyme pepsin is typically used to make digest of blood. Pepsin digests the red blood cells and the red blood cell proteins, releasing nutrients and growth factors that can support the growth of various bacteria when used as a culture medium.

9.18 a) Proteus

Proteus species tend to swarm over agar and cover the whole plate, swamping everything else that might have grown on the plate. The lack of electrolytes in CLED agar helps to reduce this problem.

9.19 d) Trimethoprim lactate

Both Thayer-Martin agar and modified Thayer-Martin have the antimicrobial agents vancomycin, colistin, and nystatin. However, only modified Thayer-Martin agar has trimethoprim lactate.

9.20 b) Butt

The bottom part of an agar slant tube is called the "butt". It is poorly oxygenated compared to the slanted surface.

9.21 a) Distilled water and electrolytes

The basic ingredients of agar media are:

- agar (a gelatinous substance derived from seaweed that provides a solid surface for growth)
- distilled water (to dissolve the other components)
- electrolytes (to maintain the osmotic balance and pH)
- a nutrient source (for the microbes to feed on)

9.22 d) Thioglycolate

Thioglycolate broth can determine the oxygen requirements of a microorganism. It can help differentiate between obligate aerobes, obligate anaerobes, facultative anaerobes, microaerophiles, and aerotolerant organisms.

For example, obligate anaerobes will only grow at the bottom of thioglycolate broth, while obligate aerobes will only grow at the top.

Glucose broth is used to study glucose or dextrose fermentation.

Selenite-F broth isolates Salmonella species.

Tryptic soy broth is a general-purpose medium for cultivating bacteria.

9.23 a) Hektoen enteric

Hektoen enteric agar is a selective and differential agar used to isolate Salmonella and Shigella.

9.24 e) Sheep

Blood agar plates typically use sheep blood because it provides a consistent and reliable medium for bacterial growth and hemolysis patterns.

9.25 e) Primary stain, mordant, decolourizing, counterstain

The Gram staining process involves:

1. applying a primary stain (crystal violet) to the specimen
2. adding a mordant (iodine) to fix the stain
3. decolourizing with alcohol or acetone
4. counterstaining with safranin

9.26 d) Gram-positive organisms will look gram-negative

If the decolourizer is left on too long, gram-positive bacteria can lose their crystal violet stain. Thus, when observed under a microscope, these bacteria will appear gram-negative.

9.27 e) No cells will appear on the slide

Heat fixing adheres the bacteria to the slide. If the heat fixing step was skipped, there will be no cells on the slide.

9.28 b) Cover the smear with the counterstain

The basic steps of acid-fast staining are:

1. Add the bacterial smear to the slide
2. Cover the smear with the primary stain (carbol fuchsin)
3. Decolourize the smear with alcohol
4. Cover the smear with the counterstain (methylene blue)

These steps ensure that only acid-fast bacteria stain red while non-acid-fast bacteria stain blue.

9.29 e) Ziehl-Neelsen

The Ziehl-Neelsen method of staining is called the hot method because it involves heating the carbolfuchsin stain.

The Kinyoun method, in contrast, is called the cold method because it does not involve heat.

The Auramine-Rhodamine method (also known as the fluorochrome method or Truant method) does not involve heat either.

9.30 a) Acid-fastness

Mycobacteria are known for their acid-fastness, which means they retain the acid-fast stain when subjected to acid-alcohol.

9.31 b) Inoculum

The purpose of the streak plate is to obtain isolated colonies from an inoculum. The inoculum is bacterial cells that start the new culture.

9.32 c) moisture from accumulating on the agar surface

Agar plates are typically placed upside down in the incubator. If plates are placed right side up, condensation can accumulate on the lid and drip onto the agar surface, causing uneven growth or contamination.

9.33 b) Flame the inoculating loop

After you streak each quadrant, you should sterilize the inoculating loop over a flame to kill the microbes on the loop.

9.34 b) Quadrant 1

Quadrant 1 should have the most number of cells because this is the first quadrant where the microbial sample is streaked. Quadrant 4 would have the least number of cells because this is streaked last.

9.35 e) Stab the agar

Stabbing the loop into the agar creates an area of lower oxygen concentration where the streptolysin O can more effectively break down the blood cells.

9.36 a) Capnophile

Capnophiles need a higher concentration of carbon dioxide than in the atmosphere. Examples of capnophiles are Haemophilus influenza and Neisseria gonorrhea.

9.37 d) oxygen

Obligate anaerobes can only live in environments that lack oxygen.

9.38 a) 10% O_2

A microaerophilic environment is an environment where the oxygen level is lower than the level present in the atmosphere (i.e. $< 21\%$ O_2).

9.39 b) Anaerobe

An anaerobe is an organism that does not require oxygen to grow. Anaerobes grow best in the absence of oxygen.

9.40 c) Cary-Blair media

Cary-Blair media is used to collect and transport stool samples. The medium contains ingredients that help preserve the bacteria in the stool sample during transport to the laboratory.

Competency 10

Clinical Chemistry

There are 37 questions in this competency.

10.1 A patient has a potassium result of 7.2 mEq/L. Before reporting the result, the lab technician should:
  a) ask the nurse if the patient is taking an anticoagulant drug
  b) check the age of the patient
  c) check the serum for bacterial contamination
  d) check the serum for hemolysis
  e) test the serum for ketones

10.2 What is the initial screening test for Cushing syndrome?
  a) C-reactive protein test
  b) Comprehensive metabolic panel
  c) Erythrocyte sedimentation rate
  d) TSH test
  e) Urinary free cortisol test

10.3 Which chemical does the urine glucose dipstick test use?
  a) Ferricyanide
  b) Glucose oxidase
  c) Glucose oxide
  d) Glucose reductase
  e) Hexichloridine

Answers on page 158

10.4 Which of these tests requires a 24-hour urine specimen?
   a) A1C
   b) Creatinine clearance
   c) Glucose tolerance
   d) HCG detection
   e) Urine cytology

10.5 Which type of urine specimen is taken after eating?
   a) 24-hour
   b) Clean catch midstream
   c) Pediatric
   d) Postprandial
   e) Random

10.6 Which test can rule out a false positive result for bilirubin on a urine strip?
   a) Acetest
   b) Clinitest
   c) Ictotest
   d) Sulfosalicylic acid (SSA)
   e) TCA

10.7 Midstream urine samples are most often used for:
   a) Bence-Jones protein
   b) culture and susceptibility
   c) mononucleosis testing
   d) pregnancy testing
   e) routine urinalysis

10.8 Which of these statements about 24-hour urine collections is true?
   a) If the container contains a preservative, the preservative must be thrown away
   b) If the patient leaves their house, they should take the container with them
   c) Night-time specimens are discarded
   d) The patient must fast during the 24 hours
   e) The patient should keep the container in a warm place

Answers on page 158

10.9 Glucose point-of-care testing screens for:
   a) glycemia
   b) glycogenesis
   c) glycogenolysis
   d) glycolysis
   e) glycosuria

10.10 Which sample is needed for a cardiac enzyme test?
   a) Blood
   b) Sputum
   c) Stool
   d) Sweat
   e) Urine

10.11 Which of these tests should be kept away from the light?
   a) Calcium
   b) Magnesium
   c) Magnesium
   d) Vitamin A
   e) Vitamin D

10.12 What colour is the urine of patients with jaundice?
   a) Brownish-yellow
   b) Clear
   c) Milky
   d) Red
   e) Straw-coloured

10.13 If a patient's urine is positive for ketones, the patient probably has:
   a) advanced liver disease
   b) heart disease
   c) pernicious anemia
   d) uncontrolled diabetes
   e) uremic syndrome

Answers on page 159

10.14 Which of these is normally present in urine?

    a) Bilirubin

    b) Blood

    c) Creatinine

    d) Glucose

    e) Protein

10.15 A 24-hour urine volume of 4 litres indicates:

    a) anuria

    b) nocturia

    c) oliguria

    d) polyuria

    e) pyuria

10.16 What is the normal range for urine specific gravity?

    a) 1.003–1.035

    b) 2.003–2.035

    c) 3.003–3.035

    d) 4.003–4.035

    e) 5.003–5.035

10.17 Adults normally produce around how many litres of urine per day?

    a) 1 to 2

    b) 3 to 4

    c) 5 to 6

    d) 7 to 8

    e) 9 to 10

10.18 What is the standard range for blood glucose levels two hours into the oral glucose tolerance test?

    a) <2.2 mmol/L

    b) <4.4 mmol/L

    c) <7.8 mmol/L

    d) <10.0 mmol/L

    e) <13.3 mmol/L

Answers on page 159

10.19 What is the normal range for blood bicarbonate levels in adults?

a) 3–9 mmol/L

b) 13–19 mmol/L

c) 23–29 mmol/L

d) 33–39 mmol/L

e) 43–49 mmol/L

10.20 What is the normal range for the blood urea nitrogen (BUN) test?

a) 1.8–7.1 mmol/L

b) 7.1–12.9 mmol/L

c) 13–21 mmol/L

d) 21–29 mmol/L

e) 29–36 mmol/L

10.21 What is the normal range for 24-hour urine volume?

a) 12–24 mL

b) 40–80 mL

c) 100–200 mL

d) 200–800 mL

e) 800–2,000 mL

10.22 What is the normal range for haptoglobin levels in blood?

a) 0.3–2.0 g/L

b) 2.3–4.0 g/L

c) 4.3–6.0 g/L

d) 6.3–8.0 g/L

e) 8.3–10.0 g/L

10.23 Which of these blood test results is abnormal and could indicate dehydration?

a) Glucose: 5.3 mmol/L

b) BUN: 5.4 mmol/L

c) Chloride: 135 mmol/L

d) Sodium: 140 mmol/L

e) Creatinine: 88.4 μmol/L

Answers on page 160

10.24 What is the normal range for fasting glucose?
 a) 0.0–2.8 mmol/L
 b) 2.8–3.9 mmol/L
 c) 3.9–5.6 mmol/L
 d) 5.6–6.9 mmol/L
 e) 6.9–8.3 mmol/L

10.25 What is the normal range for partial pressure of carbon dioxide (pCO_2) in blood?
 a) 5–14 mmHg
 b) 15–24 mmHg
 c) 25–34 mmHg
 d) 35–44 mmHg
 e) 45–54 mmHg

10.26 What is the normal ratio of bicarbonate to carbonic acid in blood?
 a) 20:1
 b) 80:1
 c) 200:1
 d) 800:1
 e) 1000:1

10.27 What is the normal range for total T4 in adult blood?
 a) 1.1–2.9 nmol/L
 b) 3.3–4.7 nmol/L
 c) 18–34 nmol/L
 d) 35–59 nmol/L
 e) 64–154 nmol/L

10.28 Which of these thyroid results is abnormal for an adult?
 a) Free T3: 5.1 pmol/L
 b) Free T4: 16 pmol/
 c) TSH: 1.5 mU/L
 d) Total T3: 5.2 nmol/L
 e) Total T4: 108 nmol/L

Answers on page 160

10.29 Which of these liver function panel results is abnormal?
  a) ALT: 12 IU/L
  b) AST: 20 IU/L
  c) ALP: 14 IU/L
  d) GGT: 25 IU/L
  e) Bilirubin: 10 μmol/L

10.30 Blood ammonia levels are usually measured to evaluate the health of which organ?
  a) Digestive tract
  b) Heart
  c) Liver
  d) Lungs
  e) Pancrceas

10.31 If a blood sample has high levels of urea, it is also likely to have high levels of:
  a) albumin
  b) catalase
  c) creatinine
  d) fibrinogen
  e) lactose

10.32 Estrogen and progesterone receptor testing are used to assess the prognosis and guide the treatment of:
  a) amenorrhea
  b) breast cancer
  c) endometriosis
  d) hepatoma
  e) ovarian cancer

10.33 Which enzyme, found mainly in skeletal muscle, the heart, and the brain, is associated with muscle damage and myocardial infarction?
  a) ALT
  b) AST
  c) Creatine kinase
  d) Lactate dehydrogenase
  e) Lipase

Answers on page 161

10.34 A patient has low cortisol. After an adrenocorticotropic hormone (ACTH) injection, the patient's cortisol levels are still low. The patient most likely has:

a) Addison's disease

b) Conn's syndrome

c) Cretinism

d) Cushing's syndrome

e) Cushing's disease

10.35 Therapeutic drug monitoring is typically performed for medications that:

a) are long-acting

b) are potentially addictive

c) are short-acting

d) have a narrow therapeutic range

e) have high rates of nonadherence

10.36 A blood sample has an elevated result when tested with the Jaffe reaction. This indicates:

a) arrhythmia

b) kidney function impairment

c) liver disease

d) pregnancy

e) prolonged hypothermia

10.37 An anti-cyclic citrullinated peptide test is usually ordered with which other test?

a) Anti-double-stranded DNA test

b) Aspartate aminotransferase test

c) Factor V Leiden test

d) Fasting glucose test

e) Rheumatoid factor test

Answers on page 161

ANSWERS

10.1 d) check the serum for hemolysis
A normal serum potassium level is 3.5 to
5.5 mEq/L. Therefore, a potassium level
of 7.2 mEq/L is unusually high. Before
reporting the results, you should check
for hemolysis of the serum specimen.
Hemolysis releases intracellular
potassium, thereby causing the serum
potassium to appear artificially high.

10.2 e) Urinary free cortisol test
There are three tests for Cushing
syndrome:

- 24-hour urinary free cortisol test
- 1-mg dexamethasone suppression
  test
- Late-night salivary cortisol test

Of these, the 24-hour urinary free cortisol
is usually performed first when Cushing
syndrome is suspected. This test
measures the amount of free (unbound)
cortisol in a 24-hour urine collection.
Cushing syndrome causes excessive levels
of cortisol., so a high result on this test
may indicate Cushing syndrome.

10.3 b) Glucose oxidase
The urine glucose dipstick test typically
uses glucose oxidase as a chemical
indicator. When this enzyme reacts with
glucose in urine, it produces hydrogen
peroxide. This hydrogen peroxide then
reacts with another chemical in the
dipstick leading to a colour change.

10.4 b) Creatinine clearance
Creatinine clearance is a laboratory test
that measures how efficiently the kidneys
filter waste products from the blood. It is
calculated by comparing the amount of

creatinine in a 24-hour urine collection to
the amount of creatinine in a blood
sample.

10.5 d) Postprandial
Postprandial means after a meal.

10.6 c) Ictotest
In some situations, urine strips can show
a false positive for bilirubin. The Ictotest
is a confirmatory test that can rule out a
false positive result.

10.7 b) culture and susceptibility
Midstream urine samples are primarily
used to look for infection.

**10.8 b) If the patient leaves their house,
they should take the container with
them**
A 24-hour urine collection involves
collecting all urine produced by a patient
over 24 hours. It is important to collect
all urine during this time, including when
the patient leaves their home. Therefore,
patients should take the container with
them if they leave the house.

10.9 a) glycemia
Glucose point-of-care testing is used to
screen for both types of glycemia:
hypoglycemia (low blood glucose levels)
and hyperglycemia (high blood glucose
levels).

Glycogenesis is the creation of glycogen
from glucose.

Glycogenolysis is the breakdown of
glycogen into glucose.

Glycolysis is the process by which cells break down glucose for energy.

Glycosuria is the presence of glucose in urine. Point-of-care tests measure glucose levels in the blood, not the urine.

10.10 a) Blood

The cardiac enzyme test measures the amount of cardiac enzymes in the blood.

10.11 d) Vitamin A

Vitamin A is very sensitive to light. Light can degrade vitamin A, thereby causing falsely low results. For this reason, specimens for vitamin A testing must be protected from light using aluminum foil or amber tubes.

Several other vitamins exhibit light sensitivity, including vitamin B2 (riboflavin), B6 (pyridoxine), B9 (folic acid), B12 (cobalamin), and vitamin K.

Vitamin D is generally considered less affected by light exposure.

10.12 a) Brownish-yellow

Jaundice is characterized by the yellowing of the skin and eyes due to high bilirubin levels in the blood. This excess bilirubin is also excreted in the urine, making it brownish-yellow.

10.13 d) uncontrolled diabetes

The presence of ketones in urine indicates the body is using fat for energy instead of glucose. This typically happens in uncontrolled diabetes, when the body lacks enough insulin to use glucose.

10.14 c) Creatinine

Creatinine is a waste product that the body expels in urine. The presence of creatinine in urine is therefore normal.

Red blood cells, white blood cells, protein, glucose, bilirubin, and amino acids are all abnormal in urine. They would normally be found in blood.

10.15 d) polyuria

Normal 24-hour urine production is between 800 mL and 2 litres. Therefore a 24-hour urine volume of 4 litres is excessive. The term for this is polyuria. *Poly* means "many" or "much" and *uria* means urine.

Option a (anuria) means a complete lack of urine production.

Option b (nocturia) means waking up during the night to urinate.

Option c (oliguria) means low urine production.

Option e (pyuria) means white blood cells in urine.

10.16 a) 1.003–1.035

Specific gravity is a measure of the concentration of solutes in a liquid. The normal range for urine specific gravity is typically between 1.003 and 1.035, which is close to the specific gravity of water (1.000).

10.17 a) 1 to 2

The normal urine output for a healthy adult is about 1 to 2 liters per day.

10.18 c) <7.8 mmol/L

The oral glucose tolerance test (OGTT) requires the patient to consume 75 g of glucose. The test measures how well the body processes a large amount of sugar. After two hours, a normal blood glucose level is below 7.8 mmol/L. A level higher than this indicates prediabetes or diabetes.

10.19 c) 23–29 mmol/L

Bicarbonate (HCO_3^-) acts as a buffer to prevent blood from becoming too acidic. The normal range for bicarbonate in the blood is 23–29 mmol/L (or mEq/L).

10.20 a) 1.8–7.1 mmol/L

The normal range for blood urea nitrogen (BUN) is 1.8–7.1 mmol/L. The BUN test measures the amount of nitrogen in the blood that comes from the waste product urea, indicating kidney function.

10.21 e) 800–2,000 mL

The normal range for urine volume is 800–2,000 mL per day. Anything below this is oliguria (low urine output) and anything above this is polyuria (high urine output).

10.22 a) 0.3–2.0 g/L

High haptoglobin levels may be a sign of an inflammatory disease. In general, a normal value for haptoglobin in adults is 0.3 to 2.0 g/L of blood.

10.23 c) Chloride: 135 mmol/L

The normal range for serum chloride is 98–107 mmol/L. A high level of chloride in the blood is typically due to dehydration.

10.24 c) 3.9–5.6 mmol/L

The normal range for fasting glucose is 3.9–5.6 mmol/L.

A fasting level of 5.6–6.9 mmol/L is considered prediabetes.

A fasting level above 6.9 mmol/L is considered diabetes.

10.25 d) 35–44 mmHg

The partial pressure of carbon dioxide (pCO_2) in the blood is an indicator of respiratory function. It reflects how well the body is removing CO_2. The normal range for pCO_2 is 35–44 mmHg.

10.26 a) 20:1

A 20:1 ratio of bicarbonate ions to carbonic acid is the normal ratio in blood. This ratio helps to keep the pH of blood within the normal range.

10.27 e) 64–154 nmol/L

T4 is a hormone produced by the thyroid gland and is crucial for metabolism and growth. The normal range for total T4 in adult blood is 64–154 nmol/L.

10.28 d) Total T3: 5.2 nmol/L

The normal range for total T3 in adults is 1.1–2.9 nmol/L.

10.29 c) ALP: 14 IU/L

The normal range for ALP is around 30–150 IU/L. Low levels of ALP may be due to zinc deficiency, malnutrition, pernicious anemia, or thyroid disease.

The ALT of 12 IU/L is in the normal range (7 to 56 U/L).

The AST of 20 IU/L is in the normal range (10 to 30 U/L).

The GGT of 25 IU/L is in the normal range (5 to 40 U/L).

The bilirubin result of 10 μmol/L is in the normal range (1.7 to 20.5 μmol/L).

10.30 c) Liver

Blood ammonia levels are usually measured to evaluate liver function. High levels of ammonia in the blood typically indicate liver disease.

10.31 c) creatinine

Urea and creatinine are both waste products that are filtered out of the blood by the kidneys. Kidney disease can cause high levels of urea and creatinine in the blood. Therefore, if a patient has high urea levels, it is likely that their creatinine levels are also elevated, due to a problem with kidney function.

10.32 b) breast cancer

Estrogen and progesterone receptor (ER/PR) testing determines whether breast cancer cells have estrogen or progesterone receptors. If breast cancer cells do have these receptors, it means the cancer is likely to respond well to hormone therapy. This is a type of therapy that blocks the effects of estrogen and progesterone on the cancer cells.

10.33 c) Creatine kinase

Creatine kinase is an enzyme primarily found in skeletal muscle, cardiac muscle, and brain tissue. When any of these tissues are damaged, they leak creatine kinase into the bloodstream. For this reason, elevated creatine kinase levels may indicate muscle injury or a heart attack.

10.34 a) Addison's disease

The patient most likely has primary adrenal insufficiency, which is also known as Addison's disease. Addison's disease occurs when the adrenal glands cannot produce enough cortisol, even after an adrenocorticotropic hormone (ACTH) injection.

10.35 d) have a narrow therapeutic range

Therapeutic drug monitoring is used to monitor drugs with a narrow therapeutic index. A narrow therapeutic index means that the difference between a drug's effective therapeutic dose and a toxic dose is small. Therapeutic drug monitoring helps ensure the drug remains within the desired therapeutic range.

10.36 b) kidney function impairment

The Jaffe reaction is a method of determining creatinine levels in blood and urine. An elevated result when testing a sample with the Jaffe reaction means the sample has elevated creatinine levels. Elevated creatinine levels indicate impaired kidney function or kidney disease.

10.37 e) Rheumatoid factor test

The anti-cyclic citrullinated peptide (anti-CCP) test and rheumatoid factor test are usually ordered together. These tests are ordered together to diagnose rheumatoid arthritis.

Competency 11

Clinical Hematology

There are 42 questions in this competency.

11.1 Which colour vacutainer tube is called the erythrocyte sedimentation rate tube?

a) Black
b) Green
c) Red
d) White
e) Yellow

11.2 What is the normal hematocrit range for women?

a) 16–28%
b) 26–38%
c) 36–48%
d) 46–58%
e) 56–68%

11.3 In what unit is erythrocyte sedimentation rate reported?

a) Millimetres cubed
b) Millimetres per hour
c) Millimoles per litre
d) Nanograms per decilitre
e) Picograms per second

Answers on page 173

11.4 What colour is lipemic plasma?

a) Brown

b) Brownish-yellow

c) Clear red

d) Milky

e) Straw-coloured

11.5 Why is ammonium oxalate added to blood samples before platelet counts?

a) To force the blood to clot

b) To lyse the red blood cells

c) To prevent hemodilution

d) To prevent macrophages from destroying the platelets

e) To stain the platelets blue

11.6 EDTA is a(n):

a) anticoagulant

b) clot activator

c) glucose preservative

d) lactose preservative

e) plasma separator

11.7 What is the term for the yellow discolouration of the skin and eyes due to high bilirubin levels?

a) Hematocrit

b) Hemolysis

c) Icterus

d) Intergeneric

e) Lipemia

Answers on page 173

11.8 Calculate the corrected WBC count from the following results.

Test	Result
Uncorrected WBC count	30,000/uL
Nucleated RBC/100 WBC	100

a) 500/uL
b) 10,000/uL
c) 15,000/uL
d) 18,000/uL
e) 20,000/uL

11.9 Which of these is a coagulation test?
a) Erythrocyte sedimentation rate
b) Full blood count
c) Hematocrit
d) Prothrombin time
e) Thyroid function test

11.10 Bleeding time evaluates the activity of:
a) factor XIII
b) fibrinogen
c) labile factor
d) platelets
e) prothrombin

11.11 Hematocrit results will be low for patients with:
a) an infection
b) anemia
c) dehydration
d) heart disease
e) polycythemia vera

Answers on page 174

11.12 Bromocresol purple and bromocresol green are dyes used to measure the levels of:

a) Bence Jones protein

b) albumin

c) globulins

d) immunoproteins

e) light chains

11.13 When setting up erythrocyte sedimentation rates, take care to ensure:

a) a fasting specimen is used

b) the ESR tubes are vertical

c) the blood is well clotted

d) the sample is completely thawed

e) the water bath is exactly $37°C$

11.14 A lab technician dilutes a blood sample with tryptan blue by a ratio of 1:1. The technician then counts 100 cells in 5 of the large squares using a hemocytometer. What is the cell concentration?

a) 2×10^4 cells/mL

b) 3×10^4 cells/mL

c) 4×10^5 cells/mL

d) 5×10^5 cells/mL

e) 6×10^5 cells/mL

11.15 Hematology analyzers use which principle for counting red blood cells?

a) Campbell

b) Coulter

c) Loughty

d) Stewart

e) Thompson

Answers on page 174

11.16 A buffy coat forms when:
   a) an SST is left to rest for 24 hours
   b) whole anticoagulated blood is centrifuged
   c) whole blood is left to rest for 24 hours
   d) whole blood is stirred with a glass rod
   e) whole coagulated blood is centrifuged

11.17 Which stain differentiates types of blood cells?
   a) Acid-fast
   b) Gram
   c) H&E
   d) Papanicolaou
   e) Romanowsky

11.18 Which of these is a sign of a poorly prepared blood smear?
   a) Covers the majority of the slide
   b) Fills half to three-quarters the length of the slide
   c) Has a consistent thickness throughout
   d) Has feathered edges
   e) Has space at the lateral edges

11.19 A patient has a leukocyte count of 2.9×10^9/L. What is the term for this type of cell count?
   a) Leukemia
   b) Leukocytosis
   c) Leukodystrophy
   d) Leukopenia
   e) Leukopoiesis

11.20 What is the term for a platelet count of 120×10^9/L?
   a) Anemia
   b) Neutropenia
   c) Polycythemia
   d) Thrombocytopenia
   e) Thrombocytosis

Answers on page 175

11.21 A deficiency of red blood cells is called:
   a) anemia
   b) erythremia
   c) hemophilia
   d) leukemia
   e) neutropenia

11.22 What does the prothrombin time test evaluate?
   a) Blood clotting
   b) Blood glucose levels
   c) Gut bacteria
   d) Kidney function
   e) Liver function

11.23 How often should you blot the blood during a bleeding time test?
   a) Every 10 seconds
   b) Every 30 seconds
   c) Every minute
   d) Every 2 minutes
   e) Every 5 minutes

11.24 In the prothrombin time test, the patient's plasma is mixed with:
   a) calcium and activator
   b) calcium and tissue factor
   c) glass beads
   d) platelet lipids and prothrombin
   e) platelet lipids and thrombin

Answers on page 175

11.25 Along with the patient's prothrombin time and the average prothrombin time of the reference range population, what other information is needed to calculate a patient's international normalized ratio?

a) The dosage of the patient's anticoagulant medication

b) The half-life of the patient's anticoagulant medication

c) The international sensitivity index of the thromboplastin reagent

d) The patient's age

e) The total thrombus volume from the thromboelastograph waveform

11.26 What formula calculates red blood cell distribution width?

a) 1 SD of the MCV / MCV

b) HCT / RBC

c) HGB / Hct

d) HGB / RBC

e) RBC × MCV

11.27 What does a wide distribution curve on a blood cell histogram indicate?

a) The blood cells are all roughly the same size

b) The blood cells are larger than normal

c) The blood cells are smaller than normal

d) The blood cells are unequal in size

e) There are more blood cells than normal

11.28 On blood cell histograms, what does the y-axis represent?

a) Cell colour

b) Cell shape

c) Cell size

d) Number of cells

e) Time

Answers on page 176

11.29 Which red blood cell index is the average amount of hemoglobin in a single red blood cell?

a) CBC

b) MCH

c) MCV

d) RBC

e) RDW

11.30 Which of these complete blood count values is calculated, not measured?

a) Hemoglobin

b) MCHC

c) Platelet count

d) Red blood cell count

e) White blood cell count

11.31 A patient has the following hematology results:

Test	Result
RBC	4.68×10^{12}/L
Hemoglobin	133 g/L
Hematocrit	0.451

Calculate the patient's mean corpuscular hemoglobin (MCH).

a) 0.035 pg

b) 10.4 pg

c) 28.4 pg

d) 59.85 pg

e) 295.6 pg

Answers on page 176

11.32 What colour do red blood cells appear when stained with a Romanowsky stain?

a) Blue

b) Green

c) Purple

d) Red

e) Yellow

11.33 A hematology analyzer has produced results inconsistent with a patient's symptoms. What would be the most appropriate action to take first?

a) Check that the test was run correctly

b) Contact the manufacturer of the analyzer

c) Inform the physician about the results

d) Report the results but with a note about the inconsistency

e) Request a new sample from the patient

11.34 What visual sign suggests a plasma sample is hemolyzed?

a) Air bubbles

b) Blood clots

c) Cherry red colour

d) Decreased transparency

e) Yellow colour

11.35 What is the normal adult range for leukocyte count?

a) 0.5–7.0×10^9/L

b) 2.5–9.0×10^9/L

c) 4.5–11.0×10^9/L

d) 6.5–13.0×10^9/L

e) 8.5–14.0×10^9/L

11.36 Which of these red blood cell counts is normal?

a) 2.2×10^{12}/L

b) 4.9×10^{12}/L

c) 8.9×10^{12}/L

d) 10.3×10^{12}/L

e) 12.6×10^{12}/L

Answers on page 177

11.37 The normal adult range for platelet count is
_____ per nanolitre of blood.

   a) 150–450
   b) 250–550
   c) 350–650
   d) 450–750
   e) 550–850

11.38 The normal number of white blood cells in blood is
between _____ per microlitre.

   a) 120 and 180
   b) 4,000 and 11,000
   c) 13,000 and 19,000
   d) 50,000 and 90,000
   e) 1 million and 3 million

11.39 Which of these results indicates anemia in a male patient?

   a) Hematocrit: 36%
   b) MCH: 32 pg
   c) MCHC: 34 g/dL
   d) MCV: 90 80 fL
   e) RBC: 5.9×10^{12}/L

11.40 What is the normal pH range for arterial blood?

   a) 7.35–7.45
   b) 8.35–8.45
   c) 9.35–9.45
   d) 10.35–10.45
   e) 11.35–11.45

11.41 What is a normal INR for healthy individuals?

   a) 1.1 and below
   b) 1.5–2.1
   c) 2.9–4.2
   d) 4.6–6.2
   e) 6.5 and above

Answers on page 177

11.42 The liquid that separates out when blood clots is:

    a) fibrinogen

    b) lymph

    c) plasma

    d) serum

    e) the buffy coat

Answers on page 177

ANSWERS

11.1 a) Black

The black top tube, also known as the erythrocyte sedimentation rate (ESR) tube, is designed specifically for ESR tests.

Lavender top tubes (EDTA tubes) can also be used for ESR tests and are now a widely accepted alternative to black top tubes.

11.2 c) 36–48%

The normal hematocrit for women is 36 to 48%. For men, it is 40 to 54%.

11.3 b) Millimetres per hour

The erythrocyte sedimentation rate (ESR) measures the rate at which red blood cells separate from plasma. The results are given in millimetres per hour (mm/hr).

11.4 d) Milky

Lipemic plasma is a milky colour due to the abnormally high level of lipids in the blood.

11.5 b) To lyse the red blood cells

Ammonium oxalate is a red cell lysing reagent, meaning it destroys red blood cells. When ammonium oxalate is added to a blood sample, it lyses the red blood cells but leaves the platelets and white cells intact, making the platelets easier to count.

11.6 a) anticoagulant

EDTA (ethylenediaminetetraacetic acid) is an anticoagulant. It works by binding to calcium ions, which prevents blood from clotting. It is commonly used in blood collection tubes to stop blood samples from clotting.

11.7 c) Icterus

Icterus, or jaundice, is the yellowing of the skin and eyes due to high bilirubin levels.

11.8 c) 15,000/uL

Corrected white blood cell count =

$$\text{observed WBCs} \times \frac{100}{\text{nRBCs} + 100}$$

The question tells us the observed white blood cell count is 30,000 and the number of nucleated red blood cells per 100 white blood cells (nRBCs) is 100.

Now we need to insert the values from the question into the formula:

$$\text{corrected WBCs} = 30,000 \times \frac{100}{100 + 100}$$

$$= 30,000 \times \frac{100}{200}$$

$$= 30,000 \times 0.5$$

$$= 15,000$$

11.9 d) Prothrombin time

PT (prothrombin time), APTT (activated partial thromboplastin clotting time), and TT (thrombin time) are all tests that measure how long it takes for a blood sample to clot (coagulate).

Erythrocyte sedimentation rate (ESR) measures how quickly red blood cells settle at the bottom of a test tube. The quicker they fall, the more likely inflammation.

Hematocrit (Hct) is the volume percentage of red blood cells in blood.

11.10 d) platelets

Bleeding time is a test to evaluate platelet function.

11.11 b) anemia

Hematocrit is the percentage by volume of red cells in your blood. Patients with anemia (a low number of red blood cells) will have a low hematocrit.

Dehydration lowers the amount of water in the blood, which increases the ratio of red blood cells to blood volume. This would increase hematocrit levels.

Polycythemia vera is a condition that causes the body to produce too many red blood cells, and would therefore cause a high hematocrit.

11.12 b) albumin

Automated dye-binding methods to measure albumin levels in blood samples use dyes such as bromocresol green and purple.

11.13 b) the ESR tubes are vertical

When setting up erythrocyte sedimentation rate (ESR) tests, it is important to ensure that the ESR tubes are placed in a vertical position. If the ESR tubes are not placed in a vertical position, the red blood cells may not settle uniformly, which can lead to inaccurate results.

11.14 c) 4×10^5 cells/mL

Cell concentration is calculated with the following formula:

$$\frac{\text{cells counted}}{\text{squares counted}} \times DF \times 10,000$$

The question says that the total number of cells counted is 100, the dilution ratio is 1:1 (making the dilution factor 2), and the number of squares counted is 5.

Inserting the values from the question into the formula:

$$\text{concentration} = \frac{100}{5} \times 2 \times 10,000$$

$$= 20 \times 2 \times 10,000$$

$$= 400,000$$

$$= 4 \times 10^5 \text{cells/mL}$$

11.15 b) Coulter

Almost every hematology analyzer uses the Coulter Principle to count cells. The Coulter Principle is also known as electrical impedance.

11.16 b) whole anticoagulated blood is centrifuged

The buffy coat is the layer of white blood cells and platelets that form anticoagulated blood is centrifuged. A buffy coat will only form with anticoagulated blood (blood treated with an anticoagulant to prevent clotting). If coagulated blood is centrifuged instead, only serum and a blood clot will form.

11.17 e) Romanowsky

Romanowsky stains – such as Wright's and Giemsa's – help to visualize and distinguish the different types of blood cells in hematology.

The H&E stain is used in histology and pathology to visualize tissue structures and cellular detail.

The Pap stain is mainly to examine cells collected from cervical samples and body fluid samples.

11.18 c) Has a consistent thickness throughout

In a good blood smear, the thickness of the blood smear should decrease progressively along the slide. This allows for better separation and visualization of individual blood cells.

11.19 d) Leukopenia

The normal leukocyte count is 5–11 × 10^9/L for women and 4.5–10 × 10^9/L for men. Therefore a leukocyte count of 2.9 × 10^9/L is low for either gender.

The term for a low leukocyte count is leukopenia, which is from the prefix leuko- ("white") and the suffix -penia ("deficiency").

11.20 d) Thrombocytopenia

The normal range for platelet count is between 150 and 450 × 10^9/L of blood. A platelet count lower than this is called thrombocytopenia.

11.21 a) anemia

Anemia is a lower-than-normal amount of healthy red blood cells. The word anemia comes from an-, meaning 'without', and -emia, meaning 'blood'.

11.22 a) Blood clotting

Prothrombin time is a blood test that measures how long a blood sample takes to clot.

11.23 b) Every 30 seconds

In the bleeding time test, you should touch the blotting paper to the cut every 30 seconds until the bleeding stops.

11.24 b) calcium and tissue factor

The prothrombin time test is performed by adding the patient's plasma to tissue factor and calcium. The tissue factor (typically thromboplastin) activates the extrinsic coagulation pathway. The calcium enables the function of various clotting factors involved in the coagulation cascade, ultimately leading to clot formation.

11.25 c) The international sensitivity index of the thromboplastin reagent

The formula for calculating the international normalized ratio (INR) is:

$$INR = \left(\frac{\text{patient PT}}{\text{control PT}}\right)^{ISI}$$

ISI is the international sensitivity index. The ISI is a factor specific to the thromboplastin reagent used in the prothrombin time test. It indicates how sensitive the reagent is to changes in clotting factor levels.

11.26 a) 1 SD of the MCV / MCV

The red blood cell distribution width is how varied a person's red blood cells are in size and volume. To calculate the red blood cell distribution width, divide one standard deviation of the mean corpuscular volume (MCV) by the mean corpuscular volume.

HCT / RBC is the calculation for mean corpuscular volume.

HGB / Hct × 100 is the calculation for the mean corpuscular hemoglobin concentration.

HGB / RBC is the calculation for mean corpuscular hemoglobin.

RBC × MCV is the calculation for hematocrit.

11.27 d) The blood cells are unequal in size

A blood cell histogram shows the distribution of cell sizes within a sample of blood cells. A wide distribution curve indicates a high degree of variability in the size of the blood cells.

11.28 d) Number of cells

The y-axis on a blood cell histogram represents the number of cells counted in a particular size range.

11.29 b) MCH

MCH stands for mean corpuscular hemoglobin and refers to the average quantity of hemoglobin in a single red blood cell.

CBC is a complete blood count.

MCV (mean corpuscular volume) is the average size of red blood cells.

RBC is a red cell count.

RDW (red cell distribution width) is a measure of the variability in the size of red blood cells.

11.30 b) MCHC

Complete blood counts have two types of values: measured and calculated.

Measured values are the direct results obtained from the blood cell counter, whereas calculated values are obtained by applying mathematical formulas to the measured values.

The measured values are:

- red blood cell count
- white blood cell count
- platelet count
- hemoglobin

The calculated values are:

- hematocrit
- mean corpuscular hemoglobin concentration (MCHC)
- mean corpuscular volume (MCV)
- mean corpuscular hemoglobin (MCH)
- red cell distribution width (RDW)
- mean platelet volume (MPV)

Out of the possible choices in the question, only MCHC is a calculated value. It is calculated by dividing the hemoglobin by the hematocrit.

11.31 c) 28.4 pg

Mean corpuscular hemoglobin (MCH) is calculated with the following formula:

$$MCH = \frac{Hgb}{RBC \text{ count}}$$

Inserting the values from the question into the formula:

$$MCH = \frac{133}{4.68}$$

$$= 28.4 \text{ pg}$$

11.32 d) Red

The hemoglobin in red blood cells stains red when blood smears are stained with Romanowsky-type dyes.

The Romanowsky stain stains nuclei and RNA blue, although this does not affect red blood cells as they do not contain nuclei or RNA.

11.33 a) Check that the test was run correctly

Before anything else, you should check that the test was run correctly. This includes checking the analyzer for any issues and ensuring that the correct protocols were followed.

11.34 c) Cherry red colour

Hemolysis is the destruction of red blood cells. When red blood cells are destroyed, they release hemoglobin, which turns the plasma cherry red.

Option d is incorrect. Hemolysis increases plasma transparency because there are fewer cells to scatter light.

11.35 c) 4.5–11.0 × 10^9/L

The normal adult range for leukocyte count is 4.5–11.0 billion cells per litre (4.5–11.0 × 10^9/L).

11.36 b) 4.9 × 10^{12}/L

The normal range for red cell count is 4.3–5.9 × 10^{12}/L for men and 3.5–5.5 × 10^{12}/L for women.

11.37 a) 150–450

The normal laboratory reference range for platelets is 150–450 per nanolitre (10^{-9}/L) of blood.

A platelet count above the reference range is termed thrombocytosis whereas a low platelet count is called thrombocytopenia.

11.38 b) 4,000 and 11,000

The normal white blood cell count in adults ranges from 4,000 to 11,000 cells per microliter of blood.

11.39 a) Hematocrit: 36%

The hematocrit is the volume of red blood cells compared to the total blood volume. The normal range for hematocrit for men ranges from 41% to 50%. A hematocrit lower than this indicates the patient has a low number of red blood cells. The term for this is anemia.

11.40 a) 7.35–7.45

The pH of normal blood is slightly alkaline at 7.35–7.45. This pH is ideal for biological processes such as blood oxygenation.

11.41 a) 1.1 and below

An INR (international normalised ratio) test measures the time for the blood to clot. In healthy people, an INR of 1.1 or below is considered normal.

11.42 d) serum

When blood clots, the remaining liquid portion is called serum. Serum is plasma without its clotting factors.

Competency 12

Transfusion Medicine

There are 14 questions in this competency.

12.1 At what temperature is the incubation phase of the indirect antiglobulin test?

  a) 22°C

  b) 37°C

  c) 56°C

  d) 100°C

  e) 112°C

12.2 Washed red blood cells are prepared by washing red cells with:

  a) acetic acid

  b) ethanol

  c) hydrochloric acid

  d) normal saline

  e) sodium hydroxide

12.3 Which blood group system is the most important for blood transfusions?

  a) ABO

  b) Lutheran

  c) MNS

  d) P

  e) Rh

Answers on page 182

12.4 An AB– patient requires a blood transfusion but no AB– is available. Blood from which of these blood types could be given to the patient instead?

a) A+

b) AB+

c) A–

d) B+

e) O+

12.5 A patient at risk for transfusion-associated graft-versus-host disease needs a blood transfusion of red blood cells. The red blood cells for this patient should be:

a) centrifuged

b) frozen and deglycerolized

c) heated

d) irradiated

e) saline washed

12.6 People with O– blood can only receive blood that is:

a) AB+

b) AB–

c) A–

d) B+

e) O–

12.7 When donated blood is bright yellow to brown, it is probably due to:

a) bacterial contamination

b) fibrin strands

c) high levels of bilirubin

d) high levels of fat

e) red blood cells

Answers on page 182

12.8 While separating the components of a blood donation, you notice an unusual green colour in the plasma bag. Which of these could be the cause of the green colour?

a) The donor ate a fatty meal before the blood donation

b) The donor ate a large number of carrots before the blood donation

c) The donor is on a contraceptive pill

d) The donor is taking a vitamin A supplement

e) The plasma has red blood cells in it

12.9 Which donated blood component carries the highest risk for bacterial contamination?

a) Cryoprecipitate

b) Fresh frozen plasma

c) Plasma

d) Platelets

e) Red blood cells

12.10 Fresh frozen plasma is stored at _____ or colder.

a) $-30°$C

b) $-10°$C

c) $-6°$C

d) $6°$C

e) $37°$C

12.11 What does "Rhesus positive" mean?

a) The antibodies in a pregnant woman's blood are destroying her baby's blood cells

b) The patient has a deficiency of Factor VIII, resulting in hemophilia

c) The patient has subtype of HIV called the Rhesus subtype

d) The patient has the D antigen on the surface of their red blood cells

e) The patient has the rhesus antibody in their blood

Answers on page 183

12.12 Type A antigens react with which type of antibody?
  a) Anti-A
  b) Anti-B
  c) Anti-C
  d) Anti-D
  e) Anti-E

12.13 Why is blood type O– the universal donor?
  a) Most people are type O–
  b) O– red blood cells have no A, B or Rh antigens
  c) O– red blood cells only have O antigens
  d) O– serum has no A, B, or Rh antibodies
  e) O– serum only has O antibodies

12.14 In blood typing, anti-A may be dyed what colour as a quality control measure?
  a) Blue
  b) Green
  c) Purple
  d) Red
  e) Yellow

Answers on page 183

ANSWERS

12.1 b) 37°C
Samples for the indirect antiglobulin test need to be incubated at body temperature, which is 37°C.

12.2 d) normal saline
Washed red cells are prepared by washing red cells with normal saline (0.9% NaCl), which removes most of the plasma.

12.3 a) ABO
Among the 33 blood group systems, ABO is the most important in transfusion. This is because people have significant amounts of anti-A and anti-B antibodies in their serum.

12.4 c) A–
AB patients have no anti-A or anti-B antibodies. This means they have no immune response against A or B antigens on transfused red blood cells. Therefore AB patients can safely receive AB, A, B, and O blood.

However, AB– patients cannot receive Rh-positive blood. Their anti-Rh antibodies would react with the Rh antigens on the transfused red blood cells. They can only receive Rh-negative blood.

Therefore, AB– patients can receive any Rh-negative blood (AB–, A–, B–, and O–) but no type of Rh-positive blood (AB+, A+, B+, or O+).

12.5 d) irradiated
TA-GvHD is a rare but serious complication of blood transfusion caused by white blood cells in the transfused blood. The white blood cells recognize the patient receiving the blood as 'different' and cause a severe illness or death. Irradiation of the transfused blood prevents TA-GvHD because the radiation stops the white blood cells from being able to divide.

12.6 e) O–
O– patients have anti-A, anti-B, and anti-D antibodies in their blood. These antibodies will destroy the red blood cells of any blood that is not O– (namely O+, A–, A+, B–, B+, AB–, and AB+), causing a hemolytic transfusion reaction.

Therefore O– patients can only receive O– blood.

12.7 c) high levels of bilirubin
Bilirubin is a yellow pigment. High levels of bilirubin in blood can make blood yellow to brown. This is seen in patients with jaundice.

12.8 c) The donor is on a contraceptive pill
When plasma is green, it is often because the donor is taking an oral contraceptive pill. Green plasma, in this case, can still be safely used for blood transfusions. Other causes of green plasma are rheumatoid arthritis or a Pseudomonas aeruginosa infection.

A fatty meal before giving blood would make the plasma milky white.

Eating large amounts of carrots before giving blood would make the plasma bright orange.

Vitamin A can make the plasma bright orange.

Red blood cells would make the plasma orange or red.

12.9 d) Platelets

Platelets need to be stored at 20–24°C, which unfortunately makes them susceptible to bacterial growth because bacteria thrive in warm temperatures.

In contrast, most other blood components are stored at refrigeration temperature (1–6°C) and are therefore less susceptible to bacterial growth.

12.10 a) –30°C

Fresh frozen plasma must be stored at –30°C or colder to preserve the clotting factors.

12.11 d) The patient has the D antigen on the surface of their red blood cells

"Rhesus positive" means a patient has the D antigen on the surface of their red blood cells. This antigen is part of the Rhesus (Rh) blood group system, which is significant for blood transfusions and pregnancy.

12.12 a) Anti-A

Type A antigens react with anti-A antibodies and type-B antigens react with type B antibodies.

12.13 b) O– red blood cells have no A, B or Rh antigens

People with blood type O– are called universal donors because their donated red blood cells have no A, B or Rh antigens. Therefore their red blood cells can be safely given to people of any blood group.

12.14 a) Blue

As a quality control measure, anti-A may be coloured blue and anti-B may be coloured yellow.

Competency 13

Electrocardiograms

There are 32 questions in this competency.

13.1 A continuous ECG monitor is used most commonly in a:
   a) assisted-living centre
   b) blood bank
   c) clinic
   d) hospital
   e) physician's office

13.2 You have connected a Holter monitor to a patient. Which of these actions would next be appropriate?
   a) Give the patient a bath
   b) Have the patient start a brisk walk on a treadmill
   c) Instruct the patient to keep a diary of activities and symptoms
   d) Shave the patient's chest hair
   e) Tell the patient to lie down and keep still

13.3 When preparing a patient for an ECG, where should you place the V1 electrode?
   a) Arm
   b) Chest
   c) Foot
   d) Hand
   e) Leg

Answers on page 192

13.4 Leads II, III, and aVF of an ECG are called the
_____ leads.

   a) extremity

   b) grounding

   c) inferior

   d) lateral

   e) limb

13.5 The right leg (RL) electrode of the electrocardiogram is
also known as:

   a) F

   b) N

   c) S

   d) T

   e) V1

13.6 Einthoven's law states:

   a) Lead I + Lead II = Lead III

   b) Lead I + Lead III = Lead II

   c) Lead I - Lead II = Lead III

   d) Lead I - Lead III = Lead II

   e) Lead II - Lead I = Lead III

13.7 Lead I of an ECG records differences between which
electrodes?

   a) LA and LL

   b) LA and RA

   c) LA and RL

   d) RA and LL

   e) RA and RL

13.8 How many electrodes does the 12-lead ECG use?

   a) 6

   b) 8

   c) 10

   d) 12

   e) 16

Answers on page 192

13.9 ECG leads I, II, and III are called the _____ limb leads.

    a) augmented

    b) bipolar

    c) negative

    d) positive

    e) unipolar

13.10 What is the normal paper speed for an ECG?

    a) 25 mm/second

    b) 50 mm/second

    c) 75 mm/second

    d) 100 mm/second

    e) 125 mm/second

13.11 A patient is undergoing a cardiac treadmill stress test when he starts showing signs of cardiac ischemia. What should you do?

    a) Ask the patient if he can keep going

    b) Do nothing and continue to monitor the patient

    c) Slow down the treadmill to a more comfortable speed

    d) Speed up the treadmill

    e) Stop the test

13.12 Why do ECG electrodes have tabs?

    a) So the nurse can write notes on them

    b) To attach alligator clips

    c) To attach the electrode to the patient's skin

    d) To prevent patient shocks

    e) To pull the electrode off in case of an emergency

13.13 Why is paste or jelly applied to a patient before an ECG?

    a) To facilitate conductivity between the skin and the electrode

    b) To prevent the electrodes from overheating

    c) To reduce the risk of damaging equipment

    d) To reduce the risk of shocking the patient

    e) To reduce the risk of shocking the technician

Answers on page 193

13.14 How long is a normal standardization mark on an ECG tracing?

    a) 10 mm

    b) 15 mm

    c) 20 mm

    d) 25 mm

    e) 30 mm

13.15 When applying chest leads for an electrocardiogram, where is V1 placed?

    a) At the fifth intercostal space, left midclavicular line

    b) At the fourth intercostal space, left sternal border

    c) At the fourth intercostal space, right sternal border

    d) Midway between V3 and V5

    e) Near the right shoulder, close to the junction of the right arm and torso.

13.16 When applying chest leads for an electrocardiogram, where is V2 placed?

    a) At the fifth intercostal space to the left of the midclavicular line

    b) At the fifth intercostal space to the right of the midclavicular line

    c) At the fourth intercostal space to the left of the sternum

    d) At the fourth intercostal space to the right of the sternum

    e) Midway between V3 and V5

13.17 To prevent disease transmission during an ECG, you should:

    a) apply plenty of gel to the patient's chest

    b) check the ground prong

    c) lower the bed

    d) raise the side rail

    e) wash your hands

Answers on page 193

13.18 In the IEC (International Electrotechnical Commission) system of ECG lead colour coding, what colour is the neutral electrode?
   a) Black
   b) Green
   c) Red
   d) White
   e) Yellow

13.19 Lead III of an ECG records differences between the:
   a) left leg and left arm electrodes
   b) left leg and right arm electrodes
   c) right leg and chest electrodes
   d) right leg and left arm electrodes
   e) right leg and right arm electrodes

13.20 In electrocardiography, what is the angle of Louis also known as?
   a) Anterior-posterior angle
   b) Einthoven's triangle
   c) Lead I
   d) Posterior triangle
   e) Sternal angle

13.21 Which lead of an electrocardiogram is needed for a rhythm strip?
   a) I
   b) II
   c) III
   d) IV
   e) V

13.22 What does the T wave on an ECG represent?
   a) Depolarization of the atria
   b) Depolarization of the ventricles
   c) Relaxation of the atria
   d) Repolarization of the atria
   e) Repolarization of the ventricles

Answers on page 193

13.23 What does the horizontal axis on an ECG represent?

  a) Blood pressure

  b) Current

  c) Resistance

  d) Time

  e) Voltage

13.24 What does the vertical axis on electrocardiogram paper represent?

  a) Acceleration

  b) Deacceleration

  c) Speed

  d) Time

  e) Voltage

13.25 The S-T segment on ECG tracing represents the time interval between:

  a) atrial depolarization and atrial repolarization

  b) atrial depolarization and ventricular depolarization

  c) atrial depolarization and ventricular repolarization

  d) ventricular depolarization and atrial repolarization

  e) ventricular depolarization and ventricular repolarization

13.26 While performing an ECG, you notice that the R wave on lead I has a negative deflection instead of a positive deflection. This means:

  a) the V1 electrode has come loose

  b) the chest leads are not attached correctly

  c) the limb leads are reversed

  d) the patient is has a pacemaker

  e) there is electrical interference coming from another machine in the room

13.27 What causes somatic tremors on an ECG?

  a) Incorrect placement of leads

  b) Interference from another electrical device

  c) Irregular heart rate

  d) Leakage of electrical current

  e) Patient movement

Answers on page 194

13.28 If there are 9 QRS complexes on a six-second ECG strip, then what is the patient's estimated heart rate in beats per minute?

    a) 15 bpm

    b) 54 bpm

    c) 90 bpm

    d) 154 bpm

    e) 164 bpm

13.29 Which of these would NOT cause artifacts on an ECG?

    a) Body lotion or cream on the patient's skin

    b) Coins in the cardiologist's pocket

    c) Electrical interference

    d) Loose wires

    e) Patient movement

13.30 An interrupted baseline on an ECG may be caused by:

    a) a broken cable

    b) electrical interference

    c) jewelry or a watch worn by the patient

    d) lotion on the patient's skin

    e) patient movement

13.31 While recording a 12-lead ECG, you notice leads I and II have a lot of artifacts. Which electrode is probably not placed appropriately?

    a) Left arm

    b) Left leg

    c) Right arm

    d) Right leg

    e) V1

Answers on page 194

13.32 What artifact is in this ECG tracing?

   a) AC interference

   b) Baseline wander

   c) CPR compression

   d) Loose lead

   e) Muscle tremor

Answers on page 194

ANSWERS

13.1 d) hospital

A continuous ECG (electrocardiogram) monitor is most commonly used in hospitals, such as intensive care units, emergency rooms, and cardiac care units. This monitor continuously monitors the electrical activity of a patient's heart, allowing doctors to respond to any abnormal heart rhythms immediately.

13.2 c) Instruct the patient to keep a diary of activities and symptoms

After connecting a Holter monitor to a patient, you should instruct the patient on how to wear and maintain the monitor during the recording period, and also instruct the patient to record their activities and symptoms in a diary. The diary can be used by healthcare providers to correlate the patient's symptoms with any abnormalities in the ECG recording.

13.3 b) Chest

Electrodes V1 to V6 are all placed on the patient's chest.

13.4 c) inferior

Leads II, III, and aVF are called inferior leads because they observe the inferior wall of the left ventricle.

13.5 b) N

The right leg electrode is also known as the N electrode (for 'neutral').

F (for 'foot') is another name for the left leg electrode.

13.6 b) Lead I + Lead III = Lead II

Einthoven's law states that the sum of the potentials of Lead I and Lead III equals that of Lead II.

13.7 b) LA and RA

Lead I produces a tracing representing the voltage difference between the left arm (LA) and the right arm (RA).

This is shown in the Einthoven triangle in Figure 2.

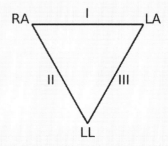

Figure 2: The Einthoven triangle.

13.8 c) 10

A 12-lead ECG uses ten electrodes. Four electrodes are placed on the arms and legs (RA, LL, LA, RL) and six are placed over the heart (V1, V2, V3, V4, V5, and V6).

13.9 b) bipolar

The six limb leads are I, II, III, aVR, aVL, and aVF. Three are unipolar (aVR, aVL, and aVF) and three are bipolar (I, II, and III).

13.10 a) 25 mm/second

25 mm/second is the normal paper speed for an ECG, though 50 mm/second may be used if the ECG cycles are too close together.

13.11 e) Stop the test

If the patient starts showing signs of cardiac ischemia (such as severe shortness of breath or chest pain), the test must be stopped immediately to prevent further complications.

13.12 b) To attach alligator clips

ECG electrodes have tabs to facilitate the attachment of alligator clips, which are part of the leads that connect the electrodes to the ECG machine.

13.13 a) To facilitate conductivity between the skin and the electrode

The human skin has a high resistance to electrical signals, which can interfere with the accuracy of the ECG recording. Applying a conductive substance (like paste or jelly) to the skin reduces this resistance, allowing the heart's electrical signals to be transmitted more effectively to the ECG electrodes.

13.14 a) 10 mm

A normal standardization mark on an ECG tracing is typically 10 mm (1 cm) in height. The standardization mark is a calibration point that is used to ensure that the ECG machine is recording the electrical activity of the heart accurately. It is a vertical line that appears on the ECG paper and serves as a reference point for measuring the amplitude (height) of the ECG waves and complexes.

13.15 c) At the fourth intercostal space, right sternal border

The V1 lead is placed at the fourth intercostal space at the right sternal border.

13.16 c) At the fourth intercostal space to the left of the sternum

The V2 lead is placed at the fourth intercostal space to the left of the sternum (breastbone).

13.17 e) wash your hands

To prevent disease transmission during an ECG procedure, it is essential to wash your hands. Hand hygiene is the best way to reduce the spread of infections and maintain a sterile environment.

13.18 a) Black

The neutral electrode is black and marked with the letter N for neutral.

13.19 a) left leg and left arm electrodes

Lead III of an ECG measures the electrical potential difference between the left leg and left arm electrodes.

13.20 e) Sternal angle

The angle of Louis is also known as the sternal angle. It is an angle found on the sternum (breastbone). It is helpful to be able to identify the angle of Louis when placing ECG electrodes.

13.21 b) II

Lead II, which usually gives a good view of the P wave, is most commonly used to record the rhythm strip.

13.22 e) Repolarization of the ventricles

The T wave on an ECG represents the repolarization of the ventricles. This is the phase where the ventricles recover from depolarization and prepare for the next contraction.

13.23 d) Time

The horizontal axis on an ECG represents time measured in seconds. The axis is divided into small boxes, with each small box representing a duration of 0.04 seconds and five small boxes representing a duration of 0.2 seconds.

13.24 e) Voltage

The vertical axis represents the voltage of the heart's electrical activity.

13.25 e) ventricular depolarization and ventricular repolarization

The S-T segment is the time interval from the end of ventricular depolarization to the beginning of ventricular repolarization.

13.26 c) the limb leads are reversed

Lead I measures the difference between the left arm (LA) and the right arm (RA) electrodes. If the electrodes are the wrong way around, the direction of the electrical signal will be flipped, causing the R wave in lead I to appear as a negative (downward) deflection instead of a positive (upward) deflection.

13.27 e) Patient movement

Somatic tremors on an ECG are caused by patient movement (somatic means the body and tremor means shaking.) They are also known as muscle artifacts.

13.28 c) 90 bpm

Heart rate = number of QRS complexes $\times$ (60/seconds on the strip) = $9 \times (60/6)$ = 9×10 = 90 bpm

13.29 b) Coins in the cardiologist's pocket

Metal in the cardiologist's pocket shouldn't affect the ECG.

13.30 a) a broken cable

An interrupted baseline is a break in the baseline. It is caused by broken or disconnected leads.

Electrical interference coming from other electrical equipment in the room would cause a wandering baseline, not an interrupted baseline.

Watches and jewelry do not interfere with ECGs so they would not cause an interrupted baseline.

Lotion on the patient's skin would cause a wandering baseline, not an interrupted baseline.

Patient movement would cause a fuzzy, irregular baseline, known as a muscle artifact.

13.31 c) Right arm

Lead I records differences between the left and right arm electrodes, and lead II records differences between the left leg and right arm electrodes. This means that artifacts in leads I and II are probably due to problems with the right arm electrode since both leads have this electrode in common.

13.32 a) AC interference

AC interference looks like a thick fuzzy line on the ECG tracing. It results from nearby electrical devices such as laptops, tablets, and phones.

Did you pass?

To find out if you've passed this mock exam, fill in the boxes below with your scores for each section. Then add up your scores for each section to get your total.

1. Standards of Practice: _____ / 20

2. Medical Terminology: _____ / 35

3. Basic Biology, Anatomy and Physiology: _____ / 65

4. Laboratory Mathematics and Quality Management: _____ / 45

5. Specimen Procurement, Processing and Data Collection: _____ / 67

6. Laboratory Safety: _____ / 52

7. Laboratory Equipment: _____ / 30

8. Histology and Cytology: _____ / 21

9. Clinical Microbiology: _____ / 40

10. Clinical Chemistry: _____ / 37

11. Clinical Hematology: _____ / 42

12. Transfusion Medicine: _____ / 14

13. Electrocardiograms: _____ / 32

Total score: _____ **out of 500 questions correct**

You've passed this exam if you correctly answered at least 300 questions (60%).

Keep in mind that the real exam will only contain 200 questions instead of 500.

Need more practice?

Get our third practice test at
amazon.ca/dp/B08YQCQN4Q

Index

Top tips for study success

1

Stay organised
Keep your study area clean and organized. A clutter-free space can improve focus and productivity.

2

Find your optimal study time
Identify the time of day when you are most alert and focused, and schedule your most challenging tasks during that period.

3

Set clear goals
Define what you want to achieve in each study session. Having specific goals helps you stay focused and motivated.

4

Create a schedule
Establish a study schedule that aligns with your daily routine. Make your schedule clear to friends and family.

5

Break it down
Break your study material into smaller, manageable chunks. This makes it easier to understand and remember.

6

Teach someone else
Reinforce your knowledge by explaining what you've learned to someone else.

7

Use different resources
Explore various learning resources such as textbooks, websites, and videos to gain a well-rounded understanding of topics.

8

Take regular breaks
Take a break from studying every thirty minutes or so. Breaks help prevent burnout and improve concentration.

9

Use memory techniques
Experiment with mnemonic devices, flashcards, mind maps, or other memory aids to enhance retention.

10

Reward yourself
Once you've finished a study session, reward yourself. Try taking a long bath, listening to music, or watching a movie.

Manufactured by Amazon.ca
Bolton, ON

45361183R00116